The Road to Open and Healthy Schools

In memory of

Thomas C. Hoy
Principal, Medill Bair High School
Principal, Charles Boehm Middle School
Pennsbury, Pennsylvania

Dennis J. Sabo
Principal, Bordentown High School
Principal, Manville High School
New Jersey

Their legacies live on.

The Road to Open and Healthy Schools

A Handbook for Change

Wayne K. Hoy
C. John Tarter

Middle and Secondary School Edition

CORWIN PRESS, INC.
A Sage Publications Company
Thousand Oaks, California

For information address:

Corwin Press, Inc.
A Sage Publications Company
2455 Teller Road
Thousand Oaks, California 91320
e-mail: order@corwin.sagepub.com

SAGE Publications Ltd.
6 Bonhill Street
London EC2A 4PU
United Kingdom

SAGE Publications India Pvt. Ltd.
M-32 Market
Greater Kailash I
New Delhi 110 048 India

Printed in the United States of America

Library of Congress Cataloging-in-Publication Data

Hoy, Wayne K.
    The road to open and healthy schools : a handbook for change /
authors, Wayne K. Hoy, C. John Tarter. — Middle and secondary
school ed.
        p. cm.
    Includes bibliographical references.
    ISBN 0-8039-6565-6 (pbk. : acid-free paper). — ISBN 0-8039-6565-8
(cloth : acid-free paper)
    1. High schools—United States—Administration—Evaluation—
Handbooks, manuals, etc.   2. Middle schools—United States—
Administration—Evaluation—Handbooks, manuals, etc.   3. School
environment—United States—Evaluation—Handbooks, manuals, etc.
4. School improvement programs—United States—Handbooks, manuals,
etc.   I. Tarter, Clemens John.   II. Title.
LB2822.2.H69   1997
373.12—dc20   96-35644

This book is printed on acid-free paper.

97 98 99 00 01 10 9 8 7 6 5 4 3 2 1

Corwin Press Production Editor: S. Marlene Head
Editorial Assistant: Nicole Fountain
Typesetter: Rebecca Evans
Cover Designer: Marcia R. Finlayson

Contents

Preface

The Road to Open and Healthy Schools is for administrators who are interested in school improvement. The work builds on nearly two decades of careful research and testing. The result is a set of organizational tools to observe, assess, and improve school climate.

We use health and personality metaphors to view the nature and quality of interactions in schools. The measures of this book are climate instruments—the Organizational Climate Description Questionnaire (OCDQ) to tap the openness of professional interactions and the Organizational Health Inventory (OHI) to capture the health of interpersonal relationships in schools. Because schools at the middle and secondary levels are different, separate instruments for each are presented. Thus four diagnostic tools map the openness and health of interpersonal relations in schools.

We begin in the first chapter with a discussion of the nature of two related constructs—culture and climate. The case is made for using organizational climate rather than culture as a vehicle for school improvement. The next four chapters describe the conceptual foundations of the measures as well as the actual instruments and their administration, scoring, and interpretation. Our objective is to make these tools accessible to administrators. They are user friendly and easy to interpret and understand. The last chapter provides concrete examples of how to apply the results of climate analysis in the process of school improvement and development. Finally, the appendixes provide all the instruments and blank profile sheets to aid in the interpretation.

A few suggestions on how to use the book should be helpful. Middle school principals should read Chapters 1, 2, 3, and 6. High school principals should read Chapters 1, 4, 5, and 6. The general strategy is to understand the nature of the climate construct; next, to be able to measure, score, and interpret the openness measure (OCDQ) and the health measure

(OHI); and finally, to provide hands-on examples of how to use this information to improve schools. We believe that there is sufficient skill and talent in the schools for the principal and teachers to work collaboratively to make their school a better place. All they need is the time, the desire, and the means. School boards can contribute the time, administrators can furnish the leadership, and this book delivers the means.

We owe an intellectual debt to Andrew Halpin, Matthew Miles, and Talcott Parsons, who provided conceptual foundations for the instruments. Our students, colleagues, and administrators have grounded our work in the organizational reality of day-to-day operations. In particular, we would like to thank Kevin Barnes, Sharon Clover, John Feldman, John Hannum, Carolyn Hartley, James Hoffman, Robert Kottkamp, Mishire Liao, Carol Mulhaire, John Mulhern, Deborah Pavignano, Thomas Podgurski, and Louise Witkoskie. Our friends James Bliss of Rutgers University and Dennis Sabo of Auburn University were a steady source of intellectual support.

A special thanks goes to Megan Tschannen-Moran, who made substantial editorial contributions to the clarity of the presentations. She is also responsible for the artwork, graphs, and charts. Finally, we thank Wayne K. Hoy II for writing a PC scoring program for Windows, which is now available through Arlington Writers, 2548 Onandaga Drive, Columbus, OH 43221. The program makes it simple to score and interpret the climate measures using a personal computer.

We encourage all interested practitioners to use any of the instruments in the Appendixes. There is no fee; just copy the instruments and use them. We ask only that you share your results with us so that we can refine the measures, develop more comprehensive norms, and add to the body of knowledge about school climate and change. We have supplied a simple form in Appendix E to gather such information. Address all correspondence to Professor Wayne K. Hoy, College of Education, 29 West Woodruff Avenue, The Ohio State University, Columbus, OH 43210.

WAYNE K. HOY
waynehoy@aol.com

C. JOHN TARTER
ctarter@aol.com

About the Authors

Wayne K. Hoy received his B.S. from Lock Haven State College in 1959 and his D.Ed. from Pennsylvania State University in 1965. After teaching at Oklahoma State University for several years, he joined the Rutgers University Graduate School of Education faculty in 1968, where he was a distinguished professor, departmental chair, and Associate Dean for Academic Affairs. In 1994, he was appointed the Novice G. Fawcett Chair in Educational Administration at The Ohio State University.

Hoy's primary professional interests are theory and research in administration, the sociology of organizations, and the social psychology of administration. In 1973, he received the Lindback Foundation Award for Distinguished Teaching; in 1987, he was given the Graduate School of Education Alumni Award for Professional Research; in 1991, he was honored by Pennsylvania State University with their Excellence in Education Award; and in 1992, he received the Meritorious Research Award from the Eastern Education Research Association. He is past secretary-treasurer of the National Conference of Professors of Educational Administration (NCPEA) and is past president of the University Council for Educational Administration (UCEA).

Hoy is coauthor with D. J. Williower and T. L. Eidell of *The School and Pupil Control Ideology* (1967); with Patrick Forsyth, *Effective Supervision: Theory Into Practice* (1986); with C. J. Tarter and R. Kottkamp, *Open Schools/ Healthy Schools* (1991, Corwin Press); with C. J. Tarter, *Administrators Solving the Problems of Practice* (1995); and with Cecil Miskel, *Educational Administration: Theory, Research, and Practice* (1996). He is also on the editorial boards of the *Journal of Educational Administration*, *Journal of Research and Development in Education*, and *McGill Journal of Education* and serves as editor of the McGraw-Hill Primis Knowledge Base Project and the Allyn & Bacon Case Series in Educational Administration.

C. John Tarter (Ed.D., Rutgers) is Associate Professor and Program Coordinator of Educational Administration at St. John's University, New York City. He received a B.A. from California State University, San Bernardino, and an M.A. from the University of California, Riverside, after which he taught social studies and English at public schools in California as well as at the San Quentin Correctional Institution. He was an Administrator and Adjunct Professor of Education at Rutgers University.

Tarter's research interests are in organizational theory, decision making, and research methodology, and his work has been published in *Educational Administration Quarterly, Journal of Research and Development in Education, High School Journal, Journal of Educational Administration*, and *Planning and Changing*. He serves as the Plenary Session Representative to the University Council for Educational Administration and is a member of the editorial board of *Educational Administration Quarterly*.

With coauthors Wayne K. Hoy and Robert Kottkamp, Tarter wrote *Open Schools/Healthy Schools* (1991, Corwin Press) and more recently published *Administrators Solving the Problems of Practice* (1995) with Wayne K. Hoy. In 1992, he received the Meritorious Research Award from the Eastern Educational Research Association.

1

Culture or Climate: A Useful Distinction

Why examine the health and openness of your school climate? What makes climate important? School health is its own reward. Healthy people feel good and have the capacity to be productive just as healthy schools can fulfill their mission of being a good place to work and learn. A school with a healthy climate is a positive place. The faculty emphasizes academic achievement and sets high and achievable expectations for the students. Teachers enjoy friendly and supportive relations with each other. Administrators have positive, collegial relationships with the rest of the staff. The principal influences the central office to secure resources and to facilitate school improvement. A healthy school has a strong sense of its own mission and is protected from destructive intrusions from the community.

When people visit a physician, whether for a regular checkup or because they feel bad, the doctor begins by taking several simple measurements with a thermometer, a blood-pressure cuff, and other devices to assess general health. In like fashion, the principal of a school can diagnose the health and openness of school climate using a few simple tools. The Organizational Health Inventory (OHI) is such an instrument. The OHI, which is analyzed in this book, uses the metaphor of health to describe the climate of the school. Its subtests can be thought of as measurement tools.

When individuals need counseling, they may seek out a psychologist. A psychologist often begins with a battery of tests to assess the dominant features of that individual's personality. In like fashion, a principal may want to evaluate the "personality" of his or her school using a straightforward measure. The Organizational Climate Description Questionnaire (OCDQ) is such a tool; it uses a personality metaphor to assess the school's degree of openness in interpersonal relationships. Openness is defined as

1

the extent to which relationships are authentic, caring, and supportive. A closed school personality, on the other hand, is marked by manipulation, game playing, suspicion, and politicking.

Simply taking measurements neither cures a patient nor a neurosis, but it gives the physician or psychologist valuable information, a window to address the problems that have revealed themselves. Likewise, just using the instruments in this book to measure the climates of the schools will not improve them. But such information will give the principal or school improvement team a way to narrow the focus of their efforts and attack those areas of greatest need.

Culture is another fashionable term used in the business and educational literature to describe the feel or atmosphere of an organization. Everyone knows that schools are different in both tangible and intangible ways. The character of a school is an elusive but powerful force, variously described as its feel, milieu, atmosphere, organizational ideology, informal organization, and more recently, climate and culture. Parents and educators use the terms climate and culture with ease, and even the students know the importance of school spirit, yet there is little common understanding of these ideas.

Why the allure of these general, abstract, and ambiguous terms? First, they make sense. They capture something real about schools; schools do have distinctive identities. Second, climate (Edmonds, 1979; Hoy, Tarter, & Kottkamp, 1991; Purkey & Smith, 1983; Stedman, 1987) and culture (Deal, 1985; Ouchi, 1981; Rossman, Corbett, & Firestone, 1988) have been linked to organizational effectiveness. Quality schools develop climates and cultures that promote academic achievement (Hannum, Hoy, & Sabo, 1996; Mackenzie, 1983). Clearly, positive climate and strong culture have become part of the effective school rhetoric and are advocated by educational practitioners and reformers to improve student achievement.

A nagging problem persists. The concepts have no common definitions. Rhetorical use has obscured their meaning. Until we have a shared understanding of the terms, how can we explain their influence on effectiveness?

Defining Climate and Culture

There is a variety of ways to conceptualize the nature of the workplace. It should be clear from the preceding brief introduction that we view the concepts of climate and culture as useful perspectives. The following chapters develop several different climate frameworks for analyzing and measuring important dimensions of the school context. To be sure, organizational climate is not the only way to view the atmosphere of school; in fact, the notion of organizational culture also has received widespread recognition (Deal & Kennedy, 1982; Ouchi, 1981; Pascale & Athos, 1981; Peters & Waterman, 1982) as well as serious attention from organizational theorists and researchers (Frost, Moore, Louis, Lundberg, & Martin, 1985; Kilmann, Saxton, Serpa, & Associates, 1985; Ouchi & Wilkins, 1985; Pettigrew, 1979; Schein, 1990). In the early 1980s, two best sellers, Ouchi's (1981) *Theory Z* and Peters and Waterman's (1982) *In Search of Excellence,* propelled the concept of organizational culture into contemporary thought as a model of effective organizations. Not surprisingly, organizational culture is now a routine part of the language of business and educational leadership. Because the use of climate and culture has become commonplace in the discussion of schools, we focus attention on each.

Organizational Culture

Organizational culture has become a vehicle to understand the character of institutional life. Concern for culture is not new. In the 1930s and 1940s, both Mayo (1945) and Barnard (1938) stressed the significance of norms, sentiments, values, and emergent interactions in the workplace as they described the nature and function of the informal organization. Similarly, Selznick (1957) emphasized the significance of viewing organizations as institutions. Institutions, observes Selznick (1957, p. 17), are "infused with value beyond the technical requirements at hand." The infusion of value produces a distinctive identity of the organization that pervades all aspects of organizational life and provides a social integration that goes well beyond formal coordination and command. This distinctive character binds the individual to the organization and generates in its members a sense of loyalty and commitment.

Organizational culture is also an attempt to capture the basic feel or sense of the organization, but it brings with it conceptual complexity and confusion. No intact definition of culture from anthropology or sociology readily lends itself for use as an organizational construct. Understandably, there are many definitions of the term. For example, Ouchi (1981, p. 41) sees organizational culture as "systems, ceremonies, and myths that communicate the underlying values and beliefs of the organization to its employees." Lorsch (1985, p. 84), on the other hand, defines culture as "the beliefs top managers in a company share about how they should manage themselves and other employees." To Mintzberg (1983, p. 152) culture is the organization's ideology, that is, "a system of beliefs about the organization, shared by its members, that distinguishes it from other organizations." Wilkins and Patterson (1985, p. 265) argue that "an organization's culture consists largely of what people believe about what works and what does not," whereas Robbins (1991, p. 572) defines culture as "a common perception held by the organization's members; a system of shared meaning." In contrast, Schein (1985, p. 6) argues that culture should be reserved for "the deeper level of *basic assumptions and beliefs* that are shared by members of an organization, that operate unconsciously, and that define in a basic 'taken-for-granted' fashion an organization's view of itself and its environment."

Although differences exist in conceptions, there is common ground for defining culture. Organizational culture is a system of shared orientations that hold the unit together and give it a distinctive identity (Hoy & Miskel, 1996). There is, however, some disagreement about what is shared. Are they norms, values, philosophies, beliefs, expectations, myths, ceremonies, or artifacts? One way to untangle the confusion is to examine culture at different levels.

Culture is manifest in norms, values, and basic assumptions, each occurring at a different level of abstraction (Hoy & Miskel, 1996; Schein, 1985). At its most abstract, culture is the collective manifestation of basic assumptions about the nature of relationships, human nature, truth, reality, and the environment (Dyer, 1985). Truth, for example, may be assumed to derive from an external authority or from a process of personal investigation. One view may result in a culture of authority and the other may result in a culture of expertise. When a pattern of shared basic assumptions exists, it defines the organizational culture. These assumptions are difficult to identify, however, because they are abstract, unconscious, and hard to confront. Schein (1990) argues that an elaborate set of procedures is necessary to decipher the tacit assumptions of organizational members. The effort involves extensive data gathering, which explores the history of the organization, critical events, organizational structure, myths, legends, artifacts, stories, and ceremonies. Questionnaires are rejected as insufficient and misleading.

At a middle range of abstraction, culture is a set of shared values. Values are shared conceptions of the desirable. They are reflections of the more basic assumptions of culture that define what members should do in the organization to be successful. When participants are asked to explain why they behave the way they do, their answers often reflect the core values of the organization. Actions become infused with organizational values such as openness, trust, cooperation, intimacy, or teamwork. Stories, ceremonies, and rituals reinforce these values. Much of the contemporary work on organizational culture is at this middle level of abstraction. For example, Ouchi's (1981) *Theory Z* describes a corporate culture where commitment, cooperation, teamwork, trust, loyalty, and egalitarianism are basic, and Peters and Waterman (1982) suggest that successful business organizations have cultures that value action, service, innovation, people, and quality.

Finally, a sharper perspective emerges when behavioral norms are used as the basic shared orientations of culture. Norms are typically unwritten and informal expectations that affect behavior. They are more overt than either core assumptions or shared values; consequently, they provide a more tangible means for helping people understand the cultural aspects of the organization. Furthermore, norms can be more easily changed than either values or tacit assumptions. Norms are universal phenomena; they are essential and pervasive, but sometimes malleable. Kilmann et al. (1985, p. 361), moreover, suggest that with a little prodding and a few illustrations, group members quickly begin to enumerate norms; in fact, they revel in being able to articulate what beforehand was not formally stated and rarely discussed. Prevailing norms map the "way things are" around the organization. For example, "Around here, it is all right to admit mistakes, as long as you don't make them again," or "We don't wash our dirty linen in public."

Each of the three views of culture has advantages as well as disadvantages. The more abstract formulations offer opportunities for rich and penetrating analyses of the workplace and seem to be preferred by theorists interested in understanding culture rather than managing it. Organizational participants, however, have difficulty openly identifying their tacit premises and discussing their basic assumptions of organizational life; in fact, they define such activities as merely academic (Kilmann et al., 1985). On the other hand, those definitions of culture that focus on behavioral norms, rather than values or basic assumptions, are more useful to people who are interested in assessing and managing organizational cultures, albeit in a limited and, some would argue, superficial way.

Measurement is the great limitation of culture as a source of guidance in administrative practice. Cultures are not easily described, let alone measured. A trained anthropologist or clinical consultant is necessary (Schein, 1985) to map a specific culture in any detail. Therein lies the rub for most school administrators. They have neither the expertise, money, nor time for an extensive analysis of school culture. Climate analysis offers a more expedient and reasonable alternative in improving the context of education.

Organizational Climate

The concept of organizational climate originated in the late 1950s as social scientists studied variations in work environments. Although researchers interested in educational organizations (Halpin & Croft, 1963; Pace & Stern, 1958) made the initial efforts to define and measure dimensions of organizational climate, the usefulness of the concept was soon recognized by scholars of business organizations (Tagiuri, 1968). Climate was initially used as a general notion to express the enduring quality of organizational life. Tagiuri (1968) explained that a particular configuration of enduring characteristics of the social system constitutes a climate much as a configuration of personal characteristics comprises a personality. Gilmer (1966) noted that climate distinguishes one organization from another and influences the behavior of members. Litwin and Stringer (1968) argue that perception is a critical ingredient of climate, which they define as a set of measurable collective perceptions that influence organizational behavior. The idea of psychological climates was introduced in the industrial psychology literature by Gellerman (1960), but other writers (Forehand & Gilmer, 1964; Halpin & Croft, 1963; Tagiuri, 1968) have also noted that definitions of climate are quite similar to early descriptions of personality types. In fact, the climate of an organization may roughly be conceived of as the "personality" of the organization; that is, climate is to organization as personality is to individual.

School climate is a general term that refers to teachers' perceptions of their work environment; it is influenced by formal and informal relationships, personalities of participants, and leadership in the organization. Put simply, the organizational climate of a school is the set of internal characteristics that distinguishes one school from another and influences the behavior of its members. In more specific terms, school climate is the relatively enduring quality of the school environment that is experienced by participants, affects their behavior, and is based on their collective perception of behavior in schools (Hoy & Miskel, 1996; Tagiuri, 1968).

Climate or Culture?

Which is a more useful perspective for the analysis of the school workplace? It depends. Both concepts are attempts to identify significant properties of organizations; in fact, definitions of climate and culture are often blurred. A useful distinction is that culture consists of shared assumptions and ideologies, whereas climate is defined by shared perceptions of behavior (Ashforth, 1985). To be sure, the conceptual leap from shared assumptions (culture) to shared perceptions (climate) is not large, but the difference is real and meaningful. If the purpose of the analysis is to determine the underlying forces that motivate behavior in organizations or to focus on the language and symbolism of the organization, then a cultural approach seems preferable. But if the aim is to describe the actual behavior of organizational members with the purpose of managing and changing it, then a climate approach is more realistic.

The two approaches come from different intellectual traditions. Scholars of climate use quantitative techniques and statistical analyses to identify patterns of perceived behavior in organizations. They usually assume that organizations are rational instruments to accomplish some purpose; thus they search for rational patterns. Their background and training are more likely to be in multivariate statistics and psychology or social psychology rather than in ethnography and anthropology or sociology.

In brief, studies of climate are concrete and deal with perceptions of behavior, use survey research techniques, employ statistics, and are used to garner knowledge to improve organizations. In contrast, studies of cul-

Table 1.1 Comparison of the Perspectives of Organizational Climate and Culture

	Climate	*Culture*
Discipline	Psychology and social psychology	Anthropology and sociology
Method	Survey research Statistics	Ethnographic techniques Linguistic analysis
Level of abstraction	Concrete	Abstract
Content	Perceptions of behavior	Assumptions and ideology
Basic purpose	Describe and improve	Provide rich description
Data collection	Easy and less subjective	Difficult and typically subjective

ture typically focus on assumptions, values, or norms; use ethnographic techniques and eschew quantitative analysis; have their intellectual roots in anthropology and sociology; and are used simply to describe organizations. There are, of course, exceptions to these patterns, but they do seem to be the dominant ones in the general literature (Anderson, 1982; Miskel & Ogawa, 1988; Ouchi & Wilkins, 1985). Basic differences between organizational climate and culture are presented in Table 1.1.

Organizational climate is the metaphor used to describe and analyze the nature of schools in this book. We have two pragmatic concerns. First, how can teachers and administrators systematically and efficiently examine the work and managerial atmospheres of schools? To that end, we provide two frameworks of school climate and reliable measures for each. Organizational climate is viewed using a personality metaphor, in which we analyze the openness of middle and secondary schools. Using a health metaphor, we examine the general well-being of the interpersonal relationships in these schools. Once the climate profiles are determined, the next question is how can one improve the context for learning in schools? These are the two questions that drive the book.

Organizational Climate: A Personality Metaphor

Undoubtedly, the best-known conceptualization and measurement of organizational climate in schools is the pioneering study of elementary schools by Halpin and Croft (1962, 1963). Their approach was to identify the critical aspects of teacher-teacher and teacher-principal interactions in schools. To that end, they constructed the OCDQ, a 64-item Likert-type questionnaire on which teachers describe the interaction patterns in their schools. School climate is construed as organizational "personality." In conceptualizing the climates of schools along an open-to-closed continuum, Halpin and Croft were influenced by Milton Rokeach's (1960) analysis of personality types.

The OCDQ was a useful tool to measure the climates of elementary schools. However, in the more than three decades since the original work, schools have changed, research methods have improved, and recently (Hoy et al., 1991), the OCDQ has undergone major revision and expansion. What had once been one measure for the climate of schools has now become three new measures for elementary, middle, and secondary schools.

In constructing the items for the OCDQ, a two-pronged requirement was used. Items were needed that had a reasonable amount of consensus within a given school, but ones that would also provide discrimination among schools. The ultimate test of the item was empirical; that is, items were subjected to numerous tests, refinements, and iterations. Answers to statements of the type used in the OCDQ are measures of individual perceptions, not fact. Consider the following examples of items: "The principal uses constructive criticism," "The principal rules with an iron fist," "Teachers help and support each other," and finally, "Teachers socialize with each other." Teachers may not, in fact, likely will not, agree completely with each other on how frequently each of these behaviors occurs. Items that survived the empirical tests were ones that had reasonable consensus. Of course, the question can be raised, "Is that really the behavior of the principal or group?" It is an unanswerable question. How the leader or group really behaves is less important than how its members perceive it. It is their perceptions of behavior that motivate action. Hence the organizational climate of a school is the faculty's consensus in perception of school behavior. It is assumed that the consensus represents a dependable index of "what is out there" and is instrumental in influencing organizational behavior.

The open and closed school climates. The climate of schools can be conceptualized along a continuum from open to closed. These two contrasting climates are measured by the OCDQ.

The distinctive character of the *open school climate* is its high degree of authenticity. Both teachers and principals are straightforward and open in their behavior. They tell it like it is. There is little game playing. Principals support teachers, lead by example, and respect professionalism. In such a climate, both the principal and faculty are genuine and open in their interactions. Teachers work well together and are committed to the task at hand. Given the "reality-centered" and considerate leadership of the principal as well as the commitment of the faculty, there is no need for burdensome paperwork, close supervision, and a plethora of rules and regulations. Leadership develops as it is needed. The open school climate is not preoccupied with task achievement or social needs, but both emerge freely. In brief, behavior of both the principal and faculty is genuine.

The *closed school climate* is the antithesis of the open. The principal and teachers simply appear to go through the motions with a principal stressing routine trivia, unnecessary busywork, and rules and regulations. Teacher morale is low. Ineffective principal leadership is seen as controlling, directive, and nonsupportive. Teachers are frustrated and apathetic. Game playing, insincerity, and manipulation pervade the climate of the closed school. In a word, interaction is disingenuous.

Organizational Climate: A Health Metaphor

A second perspective for analyzing the nature of the workplace is organizational health. The health metaphor was initially used by Matthew Miles (1965) to examine the properties of schools. A healthy organization is one that not only survives in its environment but continues to grow and prosper over the long term. An organization on any given day may be effective or ineffective, but healthy organizations avoid persistent ineffectiveness.

Using a Parsonian framework (Parsons, Bales, & Shils, 1953), the concept of organizational health was defined as an organization's ability to adapt to its environment and attain goals while maintaining cohesion. Healthy organizations achieve goals and satisfy their members' needs. The approach used to identify the critical aspects of healthy interpersonal relations was similar to that used to develop the OCDQ. To construct the OHI, short, descriptive items were written to capture salient aspects of school life at three levels: institutional, administrative, and teacher. First, relationships between the organization and its environment were considered; "Teachers are protected from unreasonable parental and community demands," and "The school is vulnerable to outside pressure." Next, administrative relationships between the principal and teachers were explored; "The principal is friendly and approachable," and "The principal schedules work to be done." Finally, teacher-teacher interactions were examined by such items as "Teachers in this school are cool and aloof to each other," and "The learning environment is orderly and serious."

Healthy and sick school climates. The organizational health of schools can be arrayed along a continuum from healthy to sick. The contrasting school health profiles are stark.

The *healthy school climate* describes a school that maintains integrity in its academic programs; teachers are protected from unreasonable outside pressure. Principals in healthy schools earn the respect of their teachers as well as their superiors and are influential and able to deliver for their teachers.

They lead by example; they treat their teachers as colleagues and ensure that there are sufficient resources for effective teaching. Teachers respond with esprit de corps. They respect each other as colleagues and hold high expectations for themselves and their students. The students in turn respect the academic achievement of their peers. In sum, there are harmonious interpersonal relations at all levels in the organization.

The *sick school climate* is attacked from within and without. Special community interest groups are overly influential in the operation of the school. The principal is impotent. He or she is unable to lead, ignored by superiors, and dismissed as ineffective and uncaring by the faculty. Morale is low and nobody cares about student performance. No one is happy. Interpersonal relations are bankrupt at all levels. This is a bleak school.

Development of Instruments

The climate instruments, OCDQ and OHI, described in this book are products of more than a decade of research and development. First, the instruments (Hoy & Clover, 1986; Hoy et al., 1991) for the elementary school were constructed to answer the inadequacies of the earlier work of Halpin and Croft (1963). The greater complexity of the secondary school required different versions of climate instruments for high schools (Hoy & Feldman, 1987; Hoy et al., 1991; Kottkamp, Mulhern, & Hoy, 1987). As the popularity of the middle school has grown, it became evident that neither the elementary nor the secondary versions of the climate instruments was completely satisfactory. Thus the middle school climate and health measures were the last to be constructed (Hoy, Barnes, & Sabo, 1996; Hoy, Hoffman, Sabo, & Bliss, 1996).

All of these instruments were developed in comprehensive studies using factor-analytic techniques, several pilot studies, field testing, validity and reliability studies, and eventually, a series of theoretically driven studies to link climate with other important outcome variables (Hoy, Barnes, & Sabo, 1996; Hoy, Hoffman, et al., 1996; Hoy et al., 1991; Tarter, Sabo, & Hoy, 1995). The results of these and other investigations demonstrate the pivotal importance of school climate. To provide a flavor of the results of this series of related inquiries, we turn to a brief summary of findings.

Research Findings on Climate and Health

How important is climate to the schools? The research is clear: Openness and health are critical for school quality. Both predict an atmosphere of trust, commitment, effectiveness, and student achievement. In specific studies, for example, as the levels of school climate increase, teachers are more likely to trust both the principal and their colleagues (Hoffman, Sabo, Bliss, & Hoy, 1994; Hoy et al., 1991; Hoy, Tarter, & Witkoskie, 1992; Tarter & Hoy, 1988; Tarter, Hoy, & Bliss, 1989; Tarter et al., 1995). The relationship between school climate and trust is extensive and consistent. Regardless of school level (elementary, middle, or secondary), openness and health foster faculty trust in colleagues and in the administration.

How important is trust in the context of schools? Our research suggests that it is vital. Trust is directly linked to school effectiveness and successful leadership. Schools with cultures of trust are good places to work and to learn. Teachers in these schools are generally happy and productive, and students are more likely to see school as a place where they like to be rather than have to be. Moreover, a culture of trust produces an atmosphere in which teachers are willing to try to improve without fear of criticism or failure. They are not afraid to take risks and make mistakes because they know they can count on their principal and colleagues for support. Trust lies at the heart of healthy interpersonal relationships. Without it, schools are subject to destructive personal agendas, suspicion, and manipulation. There is an unwillingness to rely on the authority of the administration, the expertise of the faculty, the good intentions of teachers and students, or even the general ethos that should bind educators together. Yes, trust is crucial to effective schools.

Open and healthy school climates have committed teachers (Hoy, Tarter, & Bliss, 1990; Hoy et al., 1991; Tarter et al., 1989), who share in the aims of the school over the long haul and can be counted on for extra effort. Commitment to the school is a measure of the collective identification of teachers to organizational goals and a willingness to put in the effort to make proposed changes successful realities. When schools embark on change, it is important to have as much support as possible from the faculty.

The leadership of principals in both open and healthy schools rejects close control and encourages teachers to take risks in the name of school improvement. Teachers must feel free to ignore advice of the principal when it conflicts with a professional judgment, and principals must be able to accept mistakes that come from such teacher autonomy. Teachers and principals who are committed to the organization are willing to submerge their own interests to work for the common good of students.

Schools with open climates and healthy dynamics are successful (Hoy et al., 1990; Hoy et al., 1991; Hoy et al., 1992; Tarter et al., 1995). Effective schools are flexible, adaptable, efficient, and productive (Hoy & Ferguson, 1985; Miskel, Fevurly, & Stewart, 1979; Mott, 1972). An arresting finding in the empirical studies is that although the leadership behavior of the principals in open or healthy school climates plays a significant role, it only indirectly fosters school effectiveness. As we have already noted, trust and commitment of faculty are pivotal in effective schools, and it is the principal as facilitator who brings all the elements of success together.

Finally, it is difficult for administrators to talk about school effectiveness without discussing student achievement. Student achievement is an important dimension of effectiveness, albeit not the only one. Even so, parents and reformers seem more concerned about this one aspect of school life than all the others combined. Does positive school climate produce high-achieving students? Yes. Research links student achievement on standardized tests with the climate of the school (Bossert, 1988; Brookover et al., 1978; Hannum, 1994; Hoy, Hannum, & Sabo, 1996; Hoy et al., 1990; Hoy et al., 1991; Moos, 1979; Shouse & Brinson, 1995).

More specifically, healthier school climates in middle and high schools are positively correlated with standardized achievement test scores in math, reading, and writing. High-achieving secondary and middle schools are those with high academic press and active community involvement, both fundamental elements of school health. Even controlling for socioeconomic status, which typically overwhelms other variables explaining student achievement, dimensions of organizational health and school climate are significant predictors of how well students perform on standardized tests. Regardless of the wealth of a school district, school climate makes a difference in student achievement. Healthy schools create an environment in which students achieve. The studies that link school climate, student achievement, and faculty trust and commitment are summarized in Table 1.2 for the reader who is interested in the details.

The climate of a school is much easier to change than the socioeconomic level of the community. From a practical perspective, a beginning step in promoting high student achievement and more effective schools is to identify the profile of school climate with the aim of restructuring the environment so that both climate and performance improve. The remainder of the book takes this practical perspective of change and improvement as a guide to administrative action.

Conclusion

The character of a school can be thought of in terms of organizational climate or culture. Both terms refer to the distinctive attributes of individual organizations and have a rich history in the social science literature. Culture, the more abstract term, provides thick descriptions of school life. Its application to schools is limited because of the time required, the special expertise cultural analysis demands, and the difficulty of describing the shared assumptions, values, and norms.

Organizational climate, on the other hand, offers a sharper focus on the character of the workplace. Climate refers to shared perceptions of behavior. It points to specific and easily measured attributes of schools that have important implications for both the social and intellectual develop-

Table 1.2 Summary of Research on Climate and School Effectiveness Variables

Author	Journal or Book	Variables
Bossert, 1988	*Handbook of Research on Educational Administration*	Climate and effectiveness
Brookover et al., 1978	*American Educational Research Journal*	Climate and achievement
Hannum, 1994	*The Organizational Climate of Middle Schools, Teacher Efficacy, and Student Achievement*	Climate and achievement
Hannum, Hoy, and Sabo, 1996	AERA annual convention paper	Climate and achievement
Hoffman, Sabo, Bliss, and Hoy 1994	*Journal of School Leadership*	Climate and trust
Hoy and Ferguson, 1985	*Educational Administration Quarterly*	School effectiveness and achievement
Hoy, Tarter, and Bliss, 1990	*Educational Administration Quarterly*	Climate, trust, and effectiveness
Hoy, Tarter, and Kottkamp, 1991	*Open Schools/Healthy Schools*	Climate, trust, and effectiveness
Hoy, Tarter, and Witkoskie, 1992	*Journal of Research and Development in Education*	Climate, trust, and effectiveness
Liao, 1994	*School Climate and Effectiveness in Taiwan's Secondary Schools* (unpublished dissertation)	Climate and effectiveness
Miskel, Fevurly, and Stewart, 1979	*Educational Administration Quarterly*	Structure and school effectiveness
Moos, 1979	*Evaluating Educational Environments*	Climate and achievement
Mott, 1972	*The Characteristics of Effective Organizations*	Leadership and effectiveness
Shouse and Brinson, 1995	UCEA annual convention paper	Climate and achievement
Tarter and Hoy, 1988	*High School Journal*	Climate and trust
Tarter, Hoy, and Bliss, 1989	*Planning and Changing*	Climate and commitment
Tarter, Sabo, and Hoy, 1995	*Journal of Research and Development in Education*	Climate, trust, and effectiveness

ment of students. The application of climate analysis to the improvement of schools is easy, straightforward, and accessible to the typical school administrator or school improvement team. In fact, a careful reading of this book will supply all the necessary information to map, analyze, and improve school climate.

The next five chapters are written for practitioners who want to use climate instruments. Two complementary windows for observing school climate, openness and health, are presented as aids to describing and understanding the dynamics of teacher-principal, teacher-teacher, and student-teacher interactions. Each perspective can be reliably and validly measured by a short, descriptive instrument—the OCDQ or the OHI. First, we will briefly review the conceptual foundations for each instrument; then, we will present the actual instrument to be administered and define its subscales; next, we describe the scoring procedures; and finally, we will discuss norms and the interpretation of the results. In short, we will provide all the information that principals and teachers need to administer, score, and interpret the climate and health scales. Principals and teachers will be able to engage in self-study, organizational development, and school improvement. Computer scoring of the scales is also available.[1] Finally, we will illustrate how to use these tools to develop the potential in your school.

Remember, measures of climate are measures of perceptions. They may differ, even in the same school, depending on one's perspective. Indeed, one of the useful pieces of information that can come from climate analysis is the extent to which the perceptions of the principal differ from those of the teachers. Both may perceive that there are problems but attribute the problems to different sources. Or a principal may perceive a healthy or open school climate, whereas teachers see quite a different school. In such cases, the point is not who is right or wrong but just that the situation looks very different depending on one's vantage point. It would behoove the principal who did not perceive a problem to take seriously the difficulties perceived by teachers. Discrepancy analysis provided by comparing teachers' and principal's perceptions of climate is a valuable guide to organizing information and planning change. Scores of the assistant principal(s) might offer yet another view of the climate.

We believe that these scales, either alone or in combination, can be used systematically to analyze the school workplace and to develop strategies to improve the climate and health of schools. For those interested in the factor-analytic studies and technical details of the construction of the instruments, see Hoy et al. (1991) and Hoy and Sabo (in press). We have several suggestions for readers of this book. For those interested in middle schools, study Chapters 2 and 3, and then move on to the last chapter. Likewise, if the focus of interest is secondary schools, study Chapters 4 and 5 before going on to the last chapter.

Note

1. A computer scoring program for the instruments described in the following chapters is available from Arlington Writers, 2548 Onandaga Drive, Columbus, Ohio 43221. The program, which runs on Windows 3.1 or later, will score each subtest, standardize school scores, and provide indexes of openness and health. For information, see Appendix E or fax 614-488-5075.

2

Open Climates in Middle Schools

Middle schools are hybrid organizations having the trappings of both elementary and secondary schools yet possessing their own unique structure and function in American public education. Thus it should not be surprising that the measurement of their climate is best accomplished with questionnaires designed and tested explicitly for the middle school configuration. Although the Organizational Climate Description Questionnaire for middle schools (OCDQ-RM) has the same conceptual base as the OCDQ for elementary and secondary schools, the details and some of the measures are different. Regardless of school level, however, all versions of the OCDQ have a common conceptual base along a continuum of openness to closedness. In this chapter, we provide the conceptual foundations of the OCDQ for middle schools, a copy of the instrument, and directions for administering, scoring, and interpreting the results. We conclude this section with two actual examples from the field.

OCDQ for Middle Schools: OCDQ-RM

Middle school climate emerges from joint interactions of students, teachers, and administrators. Teachers and principals develop collective perceptions of the behavior patterns in their schools. These perceptions, which give the school a distinctive character, are based on the activities, sentiments, and interactions of organizational members. Think of the climate of the school as the school's personality.

The OCDQ-RM measures principal's behavior and teachers' behavior in middle schools. Principal's behavior is examined along three dimensions—the extent to which it is supportive, directive, or restrictive. Supportive behavior is genuine concern and support of teachers. In contrast, directive behavior is starkly task oriented with little concern for the needs of the teachers, and restrictive behavior produces impediments for teachers as they try to do their work.

Likewise, three critical aspects of teacher behavior—collegial, committed, and disengaged—are identified. Collegial behavior supports open and professional interaction among teacher colleagues, and committed teacher behavior is open and helpful to students. On the other hand, disengaged behavior is intolerant and disrespectful; it depicts a general sense of alienation and separation among teachers in the school. These fundamental features of principal and teacher behavior are summarized as follows.

Principal's Behavior

Supportive behavior is directed toward both the social needs and task achievement of faculty. The principal is helpful, genuinely concerned with teachers, and attempts to motivate by using constructive criticism and by setting an example through hard work.

Directive behavior is rigid, domineering behavior. The principal maintains close and constant monitoring over virtually all aspects of teacher behavior in the school.

Restrictive behavior is behavior that hinders, rather than facilitates, teacher work. The principal burdens teachers with paperwork, committee requirements, and other demands that interfere with their teaching responsibilities.

Teachers' Behavior

Collegial behavior supports open and professional interactions among teachers. Teachers like, respect, and help one another both professionally and personally.

Committed behavior is directed toward helping students to develop both socially and intellectually. Teachers work extra hard to ensure success in school.

Disengaged behavior signifies a lack of meaning and focus to professional activities. Teachers are simply putting in their time. In fact, they are critical and unaccepting of their colleagues.

Additional Behavior Features

In addition to these six specific dimensions, two underlying general aspects of school climate have been identified. The three specific characteristics of principal behavior define a general feature of leader behavior that is termed *openness*.

Principal Behavior

	Open	Closed
Open	Open climate	Engaged climate
Closed	Disengaged climate	Closed climate

(row labels under "Teacher Behavior")

Figure 2.1. Windows for Observing Middle School Climates

Openness in principal behavior is marked by a helpful concern for the ideas of teachers (high supportiveness), freedom and encouragement for teachers to experiment and act independently (low directiveness), and structuring the routine aspects of the job so that they do not interfere with teaching (low restrictiveness).

Similarly, three specific dimensions of teacher behavior define a second general feature of climate.

Openness in teacher behavior refers to teachers' interactions that are meaningful and tolerant (low disengagement); help students succeed (high commitment); and are professional, accepting, and mutually respectful (high collegial relations).

The OCDQ-RM, then, provides a description of the school climate in terms of six specific and two general dimensions. That is, each school can be described by mapping its profile along the six dimensions and by computing the openness of the principal and the openness of the faculty.

These two general dimensions are relatively independent and are cross-partitioned to identify the following four patterns of school climate (see Figure 2.1).

Open Climate

The distinctive characteristics of the open climate are cooperation and respect within the faculty and between the faculty and principal. The principal listens and is receptive to teacher ideas, gives genuine and frequent praise, and respects the competence of faculty (high supportiveness). Principals also give their teachers independence to perform without close scrutiny (low directiveness) and provide facilitating leadership devoid of bureaucratic trivia (low restrictiveness). Likewise, the faculty supports open and professional behavior (high collegial relations) among teachers. Teachers find ways to help students on their own time, if necessary. They are committed to their students and willing to go the extra mile (high commitment). They listen to their colleagues and are respectful and serious (low disengagement). In brief, the behavior of both the principal and teachers is genuine.

Engaged Climate

The engaged climate is marked, on one hand, by ineffective attempts of the principal to lead, and on the other, by high professional performance of the teachers. The principal is rigid and authoritarian (high directiveness) and respects neither the professional expertise nor personal needs of the faculty (low supportiveness). The principal is seen as burdening faculty with unnecessary busywork (high restrictiveness). Surprisingly, however, the teachers simply ignore the principal's unsuccessful attempts to control and conduct themselves as productive professionals. They respect and support each other, are proud of their school, and enjoy their work (high collegiality). They not only respect each others' professional competence, but they are committed to their students (high commitment). The teachers come together as a cooperative unit engaged and dedicated to the teaching-learning task (high engagement). In brief, the teachers are productive in spite of weak principal leadership; the faculty is cohesive, committed, supportive, and engaged.

Disengaged Climate

The disengaged climate stands in stark contrast to the engaged. The principal's leadership behavior is strong, supportive, and concerned. The principal listens to and is open to teachers' views (high supportiveness), gives teachers the freedom to act on the basis of their professional knowledge (low directiveness), and relieves teachers of most of the burdens of paperwork and bureaucratic trivia (low restrictiveness). Nevertheless, the faculty reacts badly; teachers are unwilling to accept responsibility. At best, the faculty simply ignores the initiatives of the principal; at worst, the faculty actively works to immobilize and sabotage the principal's leadership attempts. Teachers not only dislike the principal, but they do not go out of their way to help students (low commitment) or respect each other as colleagues (low collegiality). The faculty is clearly disengaged from its work. Although the principal is supportive, flexible, and noncontrolling (i.e., open), the faculty is divided, intolerant, and uncommitted (i.e., closed).

Closed Climate

The closed climate is the antithesis of the open. The principal and teachers simply go through the motions, with the principal stressing routine trivia and unnecessary busywork (high restrictiveness) and teachers responding minimally and exhibiting little commitment to the tasks at hand (high disengagement). The principal's leadership is seen as controlling and rigid (high directiveness) as well as unsympathetic and unresponsive (low supportiveness). These misguided tactics are accompanied not only by teacher frustration and apathy but also by suspicion and a lack of faculty respect for colleagues, administrators, and students (low commitment and noncollegiality). In sum, closed climates have principals who are nonsupportive, inflexible, hindering, and controlling and a faculty that is divided, apathetic, intolerant, and disingenuous.

The OCDQ-RM Form

The OCDQ-RM is a 50-item questionnaire on which educators are asked to describe the extent to which specific behavior patterns occur in the school.[1] The responses vary along a 4-point scale defined by the categories *rarely occurs, sometimes occurs, often occurs,* and *very frequently occurs.* The entire instrument as it is administered to teachers is presented in Table 2.1.

Administering the Instrument

The OCDQ-RM is best administered as part of a faculty meeting. It is important to guarantee the anonymity of the teacher respondent; teachers are not asked to sign the questionnaire and no identifying code is placed on the form. Most teachers do not object to responding to the instrument, which takes less than 10 minutes to complete. It is probably advisable to have someone other than the principal in charge of collecting the data. It is important to create a nonthreatening atmosphere in which teachers give candid responses. All of the health and climate instruments follow the same pattern of administration.

The Subscales

The 50 items of the instrument define the six dimensions of the OCDQ-RM. The specific items, which provide the operational scales for each dimension, are presented in Table 2.2.

The items are scored by assigning 1 to *rarely occurs,* 2 to *sometimes occurs,* 3 to *often occurs,* and 4 to *very frequently occurs.* When an item is reversed scored (indicated by an asterisk in Table 2.2), *rarely occurs* receives a 4, *sometimes occurs* a 3, and so on. Each item is scored for each respondent, and then an average school score for *each item* is computed by averaging the item responses across the school; remember, the school is the unit of analysis. For example, if School A has 25 teachers responding to the OCDQ-RM, each individual questionnaire is scored and then an average score for

Table 2.1 OCDQ-RM

Directions: The following are statements about your school. Please indicate the extent to which each statement characterizes your school by circling the appropriate response.

RO = rarely occurs; SO = sometimes occurs; O = often occurs; VFO = very frequently occurs

1. The principal compliments teachers.	RO SO O VFO
2. Teachers have parties for each other.	RO SO O VFO
3. Teachers are burdened with busywork.	RO SO O VFO
4. Routine duties interfere with the job of teaching.	RO SO O VFO
5. Teachers "go the extra mile" with their students.	RO SO O VFO
6. Teachers are committed to helping their students.	RO SO O VFO
7. Teachers help students on their own time.	RO SO O VFO
8. Teachers interrupt other teachers who are talking in staff meetings.	RO SO O VFO
9. The principal rules with an iron fist.	RO SO O VFO
10. The principal encourages teacher autonomy.	RO SO O VFO
11. The principal goes out of his or her way to help teachers.	RO SO O VFO
12. The principal is available after school to help teachers when assistance is needed.	RO SO O VFO
13. Teachers invite other faculty members to visit them at home.	RO SO O VFO
14. Teachers socialize with each other on a regular basis.	RO SO O VFO
15. The principal uses constructive criticism.	RO SO O VFO
16. Teachers who have personal problems receive support form other staff members.	RO SO O VFO
17. Teachers stay after school to tutor students who need help.	RO SO O VFO
18. Teachers accept additional duties if students will benefit.	RO SO O VFO
19. The principal looks out for the personal welfare of teachers.	RO SO O VFO
20. The principal supervises teachers closely.	RO SO O VFO
21. Teachers leave school immediately after school is over.	RO SO O VFO
22. Most of the teachers here accept the faults of their colleagues.	RO SO O VFO
23. Teachers exert group pressure on nonconforming faculty members.	RO SO O VFO
24. The principal listens to and accepts teachers' suggestions.	RO SO O VFO
25. Teachers have fun socializing together during school time.	RO SO O VFO
26. Teachers ramble when they talk at faculty meetings.	RO SO O VFO
27. Teachers are rude to other staff members.	RO SO O VFO
28. Teachers make wisecracks to each other during meetings.	RO SO O VFO
29. Teachers mock teachers who are different.	RO SO O VFO
30. Teachers don't listen to other teachers.	RO SO O VFO
31. Teachers like to hear gossip about other staff members.	RO SO O VFO
32. The principal treats teachers as equals.	RO SO O VFO
33. The principal corrects teachers' mistakes.	RO SO O VFO
34. Teachers provide strong social support for colleagues.	RO SO O VFO
35. Teachers respect the professional competence of their colleagues.	RO SO O VFO
36. The principal goes out of his or her way to show appreciation to teachers.	RO SO O VFO
37. The principal keeps a close check on sign-in times.	RO SO O VFO
38. The principal monitors everything teachers do.	RO SO O VFO
39. Administrative paperwork is burdensome at this school.	RO SO O VFO
40. Teachers help and support each other.	RO SO O VFO
41. The principal closely checks teacher activities.	RO SO O VFO

(continued on the next page)

Table 2.1 Continued

42. Assigned nonteaching duties are excessive.	RO SO O VFO
43. The interactions between team/unit members are cooperative.	RO SO O VFO
44. The principal accepts and implements ideas suggested by faculty members.	RO SO O VFO
45. Members of teams/units consider other members to be their friends.	RO SO O VFO
46. Extra help is available to students who need help.	RO SO O VFO
47. Teachers volunteer to sponsor after-school activities.	RO SO O VFO
48. Teachers spend time after school with students who have individual problems.	RO SO O VFO
49. The principal sets an example by working hard himself or herself.	RO SO O VFO
50. Teachers are polite to each other.	RO SO O VFO

SOURCE: James Hoffman, *The Organizational Climate of Middle Schools and Dimensions of Authenticity and Trust.* (Unpublished doctoral dissertation, Rutgers University, New Brunswick, New Jersey, 1993.) Used with permission.

Table 2.2 Items That Compose the Six Subtests of the OCDQ-RM

Principal's behavior

Supportive behavior items	*Questionnaire no.*
1. The principal compliments teachers.	(1)
2. The principal encourages teacher autonomy.	(10)
3. The principal goes out of his or her way to help teachers.	(11)
4. The principal is available after school to help teachers when assistance is needed.	(12)
5. The principal uses constructive criticism.	(15)
6. The principal looks out for the personal welfare of teachers.	(19)
7. The principal listens to and accepts teachers' suggestions.	(24)
8. The principal treats teachers as equals.	(32)
9. The principal goes out of his or her way to show appreciation to teachers.	(36)
10. The principal accepts and implements ideas suggested by faculty members.	(44)
11. The principal sets an example by working hard himself or herself.	(49)

Directive behavior items	*Questionnaire no.*
1. The principal rules with an iron fist.	(9)
2. The principal supervises teachers closely.	(20)
3. The principal corrects teachers' mistakes.	(33)
4. The principal keeps a close check on sign-in times.	(37)
5. The principal monitors everything teachers do.	(38)
6. The principal closely checks teacher activities.	(41)

Restrictive behavior items	*Questionnaire no.*
1. Teachers are burdened with busywork.	(3)
2. Routine duties interfere with the job of teaching.	(4)
3. Administrative paperwork is burdensome at this school.	(39)
4. Assigned nonteaching duties are excessive.	(42)

Table 2.2 Continued

Teachers' behavior

Collegial behavior items *Questionnaire no.*

1. Teachers have parties for each other. (2)
2. Teachers invite other faculty members to visit them at home. (13)
3. Teachers socialize with each other on a regular basis. (14)
4. Teachers who have personal problems receive support from other staff members. (16)
5. Most of the teachers accept the faults of their colleagues. (22)
6. Teachers have fun socializing together during school time. (25)
7. Teachers provide strong social support for colleagues. (34)
8. Teachers respect the professional competence of their colleagues. (35)
9. Teachers help and support each other. (40)
10. The interactions between team/unit members are cooperative. (43)
11. Members of teams/units consider other members to be their friends. (45)

Committed behavior items *Questionnaire no.*

1. Teachers "go the extra mile" with their students. (5)
2. Teachers are committed to helping their students. (6)
3. Teachers help students on their own time. (7)
4. Teachers stay after school to tutor students who need help. (17)
5. Teachers accept additional duties if students will benefit. (18)
*6. Teachers leave immediately after school is over. (21)
7. Extra help is available to students who need help. (46)
8. Teachers volunteer to sponsor after-school activities. (47)
9. Teachers spend time after school with students who have individual problems. (48)

Intimate behavior items *Questionnaire no.*

1. Teachers interrupt other teachers who are talking at staff meetings. (8)
2. Teachers exert group pressure on nonconforming faculty members. (23)
3. Teachers ramble when they talk at faculty meetings. (26)
4. Teachers are rude to other staff members. (27)
5. Teachers make wisecracks to each other during meetings. (28)
6. Teachers mock teachers who are different. (29)
7. Teachers don't listen to other teachers. (30)
8. Teachers like to hear gossip about other staff members. (31)
*9. Teachers are polite to one another. (50)

*Scored in reverse.

all respondents is computed for each item. Thus the average score for the 25 teachers is calculated for Item 1, then Item 2, and so on. The average school scores for the items defining each subtest are added to yield school subtest scores. The six subtest scores represent the climate profile for the school.

Scoring the OCDQ-RM

Step 1: Score each item for each respondent with the appropriate number (1, 2, 3, or 4). Be sure to reverse score Items 21 and 50.

Step 2: Calculate an average school score for each item. Add all the teacher scores for each school on each item and then divide by the number of teachers in the school. Round the score to the nearest hundredth. This score represents the average school item score. You should have 50 average school item scores before proceeding.

Step 3: Sum the average school item scores as follows:

Supportive behavior (S) = 1 + 10 + 11 + 12 + 15 + 19 + 24 + 32 + 36 + 44 + 49

Directive behavior (Dir) = 9 + 20 + 33 + 37 + 38 + 41

Restrictive behavior (R) = 3 + 4+ 39 + 42

Collegial behavior (Col) = 2 + 13 + 14 + 16 + 22 + 25 + 34 + 35 + 40 + 43 + 45

Committed behavior (Com) = 5 + 6 + 7 + 17 + 18 + 21 + 46 + 47 + 48

Disengaged behavior (Dis) = 8 + 23 + 26 + 27 + 28 + 29 + 30 + 31 + 50

These six scores represent the climate profile of the school. You may wish to compare your school profile with other schools. In doing so, we recommend that you convert each school score to a standardized score. The current database on middle schools is drawn from a large, diverse sample of schools in New Jersey. The average scores and standard deviations for each climate dimension are summarized as follows:

	Mean (M)	*Standard Deviation (SD)*
Supportive behavior (S)	29.39	4.61
Directive behavior (Dir)	12.09	2.40
Restrictive behavior (R)	9.11	1.52
Collegial behavior (Col)	29.30	3.01
Committed behavior (Com)	26.76	2.74
Disengaged behavior (Dis)	15.56	2.18

Computing Standardized Score of the OCDQ-RM

Step 1: Convert the school subtest scores to standardized scores with a mean of 500 and a standard deviation of 100, which we call SdS scores. Use the following formulas:

$$\text{SdS for S} = 100(S - 29.39)/4.61 + 500$$

> First compute the difference between your school score on S and the mean of 29.39 for the normative sample (S − 29.39). Then multiply the difference by one hundred [100(S − 29.39)]. Next divide the product by the standard deviation of the normative sample (4.61). Then add 500 to the result. You have computed a standardized score (SdS) for the supportive behavior subscale (S).

Step 2: Repeat the process for each dimension as follows:

$$\text{SdS for Dir} = 100(Dir - 12.09)/2.40 + 500$$
$$\text{SdS for R} = 100(R - 9.11)/1.52 + 500$$
$$\text{SdS for Col} = 100(Col - 29.30)/3.01 + 500$$
$$\text{SdS for Com} = 100(Com - 26.76)/2.74 + 500$$
$$\text{SdS for Dis} = 100(Dis - 15.56)/2.18 + 500$$

You have standardized your school scores against the normative data provided in the New Jersey sample. For example, if your school score is 600 on supportive behavior, it is one standard deviation above the average score on supportive behavior of all schools in the sample; that is, the principal is more supportive than 84% of the other principals. A score of 300 represents a school that is two standard deviations below the mean on the subtest. You may recognize this system as the one used in reporting individual scores on the SAT, CEEB, and GRE.

There are two other scores that can be easily computed and are usually of interest to teachers and principals. Recall that two openness dimensions were determined in the second-order factor analysis of the OCDQ-RM. Accordingly, the two openness measures can be computed as follows:

$$\text{Principal openness} = \frac{(\text{SdS for S}) + (1000 - \text{SdS for Dir}) + (1000 - \text{SdS for R})}{3}$$

$$\text{Teacher openness} = \frac{(\text{SdS for Col}) + (\text{SdS for Com}) + (1000 - \text{SdS for Dis})}{3}$$

These openness indexes are interpreted the same way as the subtest scores; that is, the mean of the "average" school is 500. Thus a score of 650 on teacher openness represents a highly open faculty, one that is one and one half standard deviations above the average school.

Table 2.3 Prototypic Profiles of Middle School Climate Types

Climate Dimension	Open Climate	Engaged Climate	Disengaged Climate	Closed Climate
Supportive	618 (VH)	376 (VL)	553 (H)	393 (VL)
Directive	394 (VL)	591 (H)	444 (L)	606 (VH)
Restrictive	425 (L)	551 (H)	437 (L)	624 (VH)
Collegial	604 (VH)	635 (VH)	450 (L)	371 (VL)
Committed	622 (VH)	588 (H)	411 (L)	421 (L)
Disengaged	409 (L)	442 (L)	587 (H)	594 (H)
Principal openness	600 (H)	411 (L)	557 (H)	388 (VL)
Teacher openness	606 (VH)	594 (H)	425 (L)	399 (VL)
Total	1206	1005	982	787

VH = very high; H = high; L = low; VL = very low.

Prototypic profiles of climates have been constructed using the normative data from the New Jersey sample of middle schools (see Table 2.3). Therefore, you can examine the fit of your own school climate to the four prototypes. Compare the standardized scores of your school with each of the prototypes in Table 2.3 to determine which of the four climate types the school most closely resembles. Note that a given school can be described by one or two indexes. A total score of 1150 or more is almost certain to be the mark of a school with an open climate. By the same token, a school with a score below 850 will have a closed climate. Most school scores, however, fall between these extremes and can only be diagnosed by carefully comparing all elements of the climate with the four prototypes. We recommend using all six dimensions of OCDQ-RM to gain a finely tuned picture of school climate.

An Example

Recently, we assessed the climate of several middle schools. The OCDQ-RM was administered to the teachers at a faculty meeting. The data were then returned to us, and using the procedures described above, we scored and analyzed the climate of the schools. School data can be scored by our computer program, which includes a comparison of your school with the normative sample and classifies the climate.[2] Two of the schools, Wilson and Frost, serve as our examples.[3]

The scores have been standardized so that the average score for an elementary school in the sample is 500 and the standard deviation is 100. We have done this for two reasons. First, the scores are easily compared with others in the sample, and second, their interpretation is not unlike that of SAT scores, scores with which most teachers and administrators are familiar. For example, a score of 600 on the Supportive Principal Behavior scale is one standard deviation above all the schools in the sample, a relatively high score. Similarly, a score of 500 represents a school that is average in comparison to others, whereas a 400 indicates a school one standard deviation below the average school scores, a relatively low score. We have changed the numbers into categories ranging from high to low by using the following conversion table:

Above 600	Very high
551-600	High
525-550	Above average
511-524	Slightly above average
490-510	Average
476-489	Slightly below average
450-475	Below average
400-449	Low
Below 400	Very low

The climate profiles for Wilson and Frost and a brief sketch of the climate of each school are given below.

The climate of Wilson Middle School is open (see Figure 2.2). Teachers are highly professional in their interactions with each other and respect the work of their colleagues (high on collegiality). They also demonstrate a strong commitment to students (high on commitment); they are willing to go the extra mile in helping students achieve. Teachers are typically tolerant and engaged in meaningful professional activities (low disengagement). There is also substantial openness of the principal's behavior (high). The principal is more supportive of teachers than most middle school principals (high on supportive behavior). Moreover, the principal neither controls teachers tightly nor monitors their actions closely, but rather gives them considerable autonomy (low directive behavior). Finally, the principal facilitates teacher activity by not burdening them with busywork or other administrative trivia that shift their attention from the teaching-learning process (low restrictive behavior). In brief, both the behavior of the principal and teachers is open.

Let's examine Figure 2.3, the climate-openness profile of Frost Middle School, one of the most closed climates that we have encountered. The principal does not support the teachers (low supportive behavior); rather, this principal spends most of the time ordering people around and watching them carefully (high directive behavior). Such close supervision is complemented by a mountain of paperwork and administrative trivia (high restrictive behavior). Teachers are not engaged in productive group efforts with either the principal or other faculty members (high disengagement). Moreover, they are not particularly accessible to students: They don't

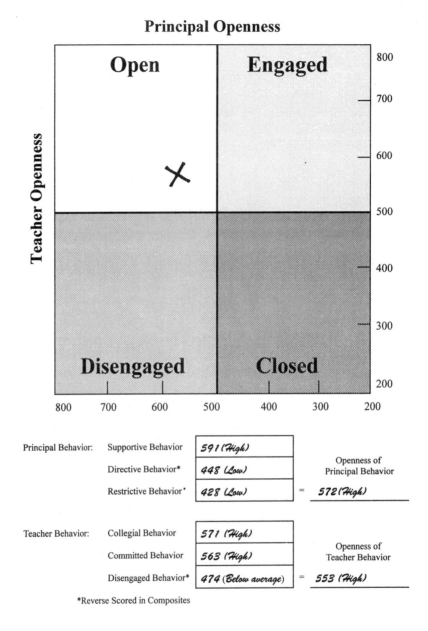

Figure 2.2. Organizational Climate Description Questionnaire for Middle Schools (OCDQ-RM): Wilson Middle School

volunteer extra effort and they don't go out of their way to help students (low committed behavior). Similarly, they don't like and support each other (low collegial behavior). This is not a good place for teachers or students. In a word, it is closed.

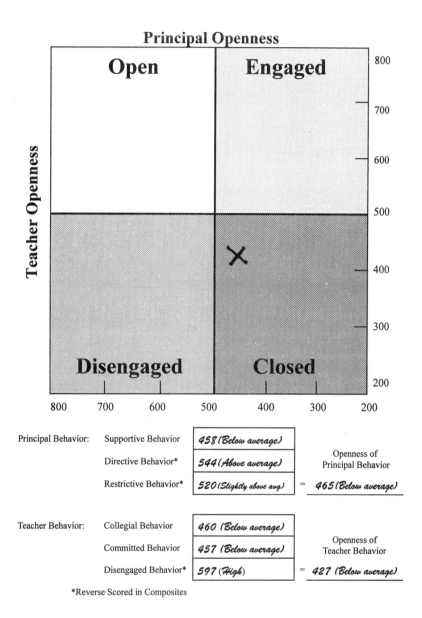

Figure 2.3. Organizational Climate Description Questionnaire for Middle Schools (OCDQ-RM): Frost Middle School

The contrast between these two schools is arresting. Wilson is a good place to work. The principal's leadership is enlightened, and the faculty respond as professionals; they are committed to the task at hand and supportive of each other as well as the principal. The interpersonal relationships are genuine. When the principal does criticize, it is for a constructive purpose and the teachers accept that. This is not a school to be tinkered with; the work environment complements the teaching-learning task.

Frost, by comparison, is a dismal place to teach or to practice administration. Suspicion and turmoil pervade the halls and classrooms of this school. Attempts by the principal to lead are direct, restrictive, and ineffective. The principal is not there to be supportive. Rules, regulations, and busywork are substitutes for active educational leadership. Teachers respond by disengaging from the collective task. They are not friendly with each other, and they don't support each other. Even the students lose out. Teachers not only avoid their colleagues and administrators, but they also have little time for students. There is no quick fix here, but it is in everyone's best interest to change the climate of the school.

Conclusion

This chapter is a lean description of the OCDQ-RM and how to administer and use it. Copy the instrument, administer it, and score it. For a clean copy of the OCDQ-RM, see Appendix A. There is no copyright restriction for noncommercial use by schools; feel free to make as many copies as you wish. Then determine your school's climate profile and evaluate the openness of the climate. Do you want to improve or change the climate? Before you engage in a school improvement plan, we suggest you assess the organizational health of a school (Chapter 3). With both openness and health profiles in hand and knowledge of your own school, you are in a better position to plan change. Read Chapter 6 for some specific advice.

Notes

1. Information on the reliability and validity of the OCDQ-RM is reported in detail in Hoy, Barnes, and Sabo (1996) and Hoy, Hoffman, Sabo, and Bliss (1996).

2. Computer scoring programs for both the OCDQ-RM and the OHI-M (see next chapter) are available from Arlington Writers, 2548 Onandaga Drive, Columbus, Ohio 43221. The programs, which run on Windows 3.1 or later, will score each subtest, standardize school scores, and provide indexes of openness and health. Further information on the scoring program can be obtained from Arlington Writers (fax 614-488-5075) or see Appendix E.

3. The names of the schools and principals used throughout this book are pseudonyms.

3

Healthy Climates in Middle Schools

The Organizational Health Inventory (OHI) is another instrument to assess the climate of schools. The inventory in this chapter was especially developed and tested for middle schools (OHI-M); it describes the health of interpersonal relations in schools among students, teachers, administrators, and community members. In the following pages, we will briefly sketch the conceptual foundations of the OHI-M, provide the actual questionnaire for use in schools, specify the scoring procedures, and discuss the analysis and interpretation of the results.

OHI for Middle Schools: OHI-M

A healthy school is one in which the institutional, administrative, and teacher levels are in harmony, and the school meets functional needs as it successfully copes with disruptive external forces and directs its energies toward its mission. Health is conceptualized at three levels: institutional, administrative, and teacher. Dimensions of health were selected to represent the basic needs of schools: to adapt to environmental demands, achieve goals, satisfy participant needs, and create a cohesive community.

The *institutional level* connects the school with its environment. Schools need legitimacy and support from the community. A dimension called institutional integrity was conceived of as the ability of the school to remain relatively independent from vested interests. Both administrators and teachers need backing to perform their functions relatively unfettered by individuals and groups outside the school.

The *administrative level* controls the internal managerial function of the organization; principals are the administrative officers of the school. They allocate resources and coordinate the work effort. They must find ways to set the tone for high performance by letting people know what is expected of them in ways that are friendly and guided by professionalism. Principal influence and resource support are basic leadership activities that ensure the presence of adequate instructional materials and resources requested by teachers.

The *teacher level* of the school is concerned with the teaching-learning process. The primary function of the school is to produce educated students. Moreover, teachers and supervisors have immediate responsibility for solving the problems associated with effective learning and teaching. Teacher affiliation, a key mechanism for integrating school life, reflects a cohesive work unit that is committed equally to colleagues and students. Academic emphasis, the school's press for achievement, is the setting of high but achievable student goals and a dedication of both students and teachers to academic excellence. These fundamental features of school health are summarized as follows.

Institutional Level

Institutional integrity is the degree to which the school can cope with its environment in a way that maintains the educational integrity of its programs. Teachers are protected from unreasonable community and parental demands.

Administrative Level

Collegial leadership is principal behavior that is friendly, supportive, open, and guided by norms of equality. But at the same time, the principal sets the tone for high performance by letting people know what is expected of them.

Principal influence is the principal's ability to influence the action of superiors. Influential principals are persuasive with superiors, get additional consideration, and proceed relatively unimpeded by the hierarchy.

Resource support is the extent to which classroom supplies and instructional materials are readily available; in fact, even extra materials are supplied if requested.

Teacher Level

Teacher affiliation is a sense of friendliness and strong affiliation with the school. Teachers feel good about each other, their job, and their students. They are committed to both their students and their colleagues and accomplish their jobs with enthusiasm.

Academic emphasis is the extent to which the school is driven by a quest for academic excellence. High but achievable academic goals are set for students, the learning environment is orderly and serious, teachers believe in their students' ability to achieve, and students work hard and respect those who do well academically.

A healthy school is one in which the teacher, administrative, and institutional levels are in harmony. The school meets its needs of adaptation, goal achievement, participant satisfaction, and group cohesiveness as it successfully copes with disruptive external forces and continues its mission. School health captures the positive contribution of all six dimensions. Brief vignettes of the healthy and sick school are now described.

Healthy School

A healthy school is characterized by student, teacher, and principal behavior that is harmonious and works toward instructional success. Teachers like their colleagues, their school, their job, and their students (high teacher affiliation), and they are driven by a quest for academic excellence. Teachers believe in themselves and their students; consequently, they set high but achievable goals. The learning environment is serious and orderly, and students work hard and respect others who do well academically (high academic emphasis). Principal behavior is also healthy, that is, friendly, open, egalitarian, and supportive. Such principals expect the best from teachers (high collegial leadership). Principals get teachers the resources they need to do the job (high resource support) and are also influential with superiors (high principal influence); they go to bat for their teachers. Finally, a healthy school has high institutional integrity; teachers are protected from unreasonable and hostile outside forces.

Sick School

A sick school is vulnerable to destructive outside forces. Teachers and administrators are bombarded by unreasonable parental demands, and the school is buffeted by the whims of the public (low institutional integrity). The school is without an effective principal. The principal provides little direction or structure and exhibits scant encouragement for teachers (low collegial leadership) and has negligible clout with superiors (low influence). Teachers don't like their colleagues or their jobs. They act aloof, suspicious, and defensive (low teacher affiliation). Instructional materials, supplies, and supplementary materials are not available when needed (low resource support). Finally, there is minimal press for academic excellence. Neither

teachers nor students take academic life seriously; in fact, academically oriented students are ridiculed by their peers and viewed by their teachers as threats (low academic emphasis).

The OHI-M Form

The OHI-M is a 45-item questionnaire on which educators are asked to describe the extent to which specific behavior patterns occur in the school.[1] The responses vary along a 4-point scale defined by the categories *rarely occurs, sometimes occurs, often occurs,* and *very frequently occurs.* The entire instrument as it is administered to teachers is presented in Table 3.1.

Administering the Instrument

The OHI-M is best administered as part of a faculty meeting. It is important to guarantee the anonymity of the teacher respondent; teachers are not asked to sign the questionnaire and no identifying code is placed on the form. Most teachers do not object to responding to the instrument, which takes less than 10 minutes to complete. We recommend that someone other than an administrator collect the data. It is important to create a nonthreatening atmosphere in which teachers give candid responses. All of the health instruments follow the same pattern of administration.

The Subscales

After the 45-item instrument is administered to the faculty, the items for each scale are scored. The items for each scale are presented in Table 3.2.

The items are scored by assigning 1 to *rarely occurs,* 2 to *sometimes occurs,* 3 to *often occurs,* and 4 to *very frequently occurs.* When an item is reversed scored (noted by an asterisk in Table 3.2), *rarely occurs* receives a 4, *sometimes occurs* a 3, and so on. Each item is scored for each respondent, and then an average school score for *each item* is computed by averaging the item responses across the school; remember, the school is the unit of analysis. The average school scores for the items comprising each subtest are added to yield school subtest scores. The six subtest scores represent the health profile for the school. For example, if School A has 50 teachers responding to the OHI-M, each individual questionnaire is scored and then average score for all respondents is computed for each item. Thus the average score for the 50 teachers is calculated for Item 1, then Item 2, and so on. The average school scores for the items defining each subtest are added to yield school subtest scores. The six subtest scores represent the health profile for the school.

Table 3.1 OHI-M

Directions: The following are statements about your school. Please indicate the extent to which each statement characterizes your school by circling the appropriate response.

RO = rarely occurs; SO = sometimes occurs; O = often occurs; VFO = very frequently occurs

1. The principal explores all sides of topics and admits that other options exist.	RO SO O VFO
2. Students make provisions to acquire extra help from teachers.	RO SO O VFO
3. The principal gets what he or she asks for from superiors.	RO SO O VFO
4. The principal discusses classroom issues with teachers.	RO SO O VFO
5. The principal accepts questions without appearing to snub or quash the teacher.	RO SO O VFO
6. Extra materials are available if requested.	RO SO O VFO
7. Students neglect to complete homework.	RO SO O VFO
8. The school is vulnerable to outside pressures.	RO SO O VFO
9. The principal is able to influence the actions of his or her superiors.	RO SO O VFO
10. The principal treats all faculty members as his or her equal.	RO SO O VFO
11. Teachers are provided with adequate materials for their classrooms.	RO SO O VFO
12. Teachers in this school like each other.	RO SO O VFO
13. Community demands are accepted even when they are not consistent with the educational program.	RO SO O VFO
14. The principal lets faculty know what is expected of them.	RO SO O VFO
15. Teachers receive necessary classroom supplies.	RO SO O VFO
16. Students respect others who get good grades.	RO SO O VFO
17. Good grades are important to the students of this school.	RO SO O VFO
18. Teachers feel pressure from the community.	RO SO O VFO
19. The principal's recommendations are given serious consideration by his or her superiors.	RO SO O VFO
20. Supplementary materials are available for classroom use.	RO SO O VFO
21. Teachers exhibit friendliness to each other.	RO SO O VFO
22. Students seek extra work so they can get good grades.	RO SO O VFO
23. Select citizen groups are influential with the board.	RO SO O VFO
24. The principal looks out for the personal welfare of faculty members.	RO SO O VFO
25. The school is open to the whims of the public.	RO SO O VFO
26. A few vocal parents can change school policy.	RO SO O VFO
27. Students try hard to improve on previous work.	RO SO O VFO
28. Teachers accomplish their jobs with enthusiasm.	RO SO O VFO
29. The learning environment is orderly and serious.	RO SO O VFO
30. The principal is friendly and approachable.	RO SO O VFO
31. Teachers show commitment to their students.	RO SO O VFO
32. Teachers are indifferent to each other.	RO SO O VFO
33. Teachers are protected from unreasonable community and parental demands.	RO SO O VFO
34. The principal is able to work well with the superintendent.	RO SO O VFO
35. The principal is willing to make changes.	RO SO O VFO
36. Teachers have access to needed instructional materials.	RO SO O VFO
37. Teachers in this school are cool and aloof to each other.	RO SO O VFO
38. Teachers in this school believe that their students have the ability to achieve academically.	RO SO O VFO

(continued on the next page)

Table 3.1 Continued

39. The principal is understanding when personal concerns cause teachers to arrive late or leave early.	RO SO O VFO
40. Our school gets its fair share of resources from the district.	RO SO O VFO
41. The principal is rebuffed by the superintendent.	RO SO O VFO
42. Teachers volunteer to help each other.	RO SO O VFO
43. The principal is effective in securing the superintendent's approval for new programs or activities.	RO SO O VFO
44. Academically oriented students in this school are ridiculed by their peers.	RO SO O VFO
45. Teachers do favors for each other.	RO SO O VFO

SOURCE: Kevin M. Barnes, *The Organizational Health of Middle Schools, Trust, and Decision Participation.* (Unpublished doctoral dissertation, Rutgers University, New Brunswick, New Jersey, 1994.) Used with permission.

Table 3.2 Items That Compose the Six Subtests of the OHI-M

Institutional level

Institutional integrity items	*Questionnaire no.*
*1. The school is vulnerable to outside pressures.	(8)
*2. Community demands are accepted even when they are not consistent with the educational program.	(13)
*3. Teachers feel pressure from the community.	(18)
*4. Select citizen groups are influential with the board.	(23)
*5. The school is open to the whims of the public.	(25)
*6. A few vocal parents can change school policy.	(26)
7. Teachers are protected from unreasonable community and parental demands.	(33)

Administrative level

Collegial leadership items	*Questionnaire no.*
1. The principal explores all sides of topics and admits that other opinions exist.	(1)
2. The principal discusses classroom issues with teachers.	(4)
3. The principal accepts questions without appearing to snub or quash the teacher.	(5)
4. The principal treats all faculty members as his or her equal.	(10)
5. The principal lets faculty know what is expected of them.	(14)
6. The principal looks out for the personal welfare of faculty members.	(24)
7. The principal is friendly and approachable.	(30)
8. The principal is willing to make changes.	(35)
9. The principal is understanding when personal concerns cause teachers to arrive late or leave early.	(39)

Table 3.2 Continued

Principal influence items	*Questionnaire no.*
1. The principal gets what he or she asks for from superiors.	(3)
2. The principal is able to influence the actions of his or her superiors.	(9)
3. The principal's recommendations are given serious consideration by his or her superiors.	(19)
4. The principal is able to work well with the superintendent.	(34)
*5. The principal is rebuffed by the superintendent.	(41)
6. The principal is effective in securing the superintendent's approval for new programs and activities.	(43)

Resource support items	*Questionnaire no.*
1. Extra materials are available if requested.	(6)
2. Teachers are provided with adequate materials for their classrooms.	(11)
3. Teachers receive necessary classroom supplies.	(15)
4. Supplementary materials are available for classroom use.	(20)
5. Teachers have access to instructional material.	(36)
6. Our school gets its fair share of resources from the district.	(40)

Teacher level

Teacher affiliation items	*Questionnaire no.*
1. Teachers in the school like each other.	(12)
2. Teachers exhibit friendliness to each other.	(21)
3. Teachers accomplish their jobs with enthusiasm.	(28)
4. Teachers show commitment to their students.	(31)
*5. Teachers are indifferent to each other.	(32)
*6. Teachers in this school are cool and aloof to each other.	(37)
7. Teachers volunteer to help each other.	(42)
8. Teachers do favors for each other.	(45)

Academic emphasis items	*Questionnaire no.*
1. Students make provisions for acquire extra help from teachers.	(2)
*2. Students neglect to complete homework.	(7)
3. Students respect others who get good grades.	(16)
4. Good grades are important to the students of this school.	(17)
5. Students seek extra work so they can get good grades.	(22)
6. Students try hard to improve on previous work.	(27)
7. The learning environment is orderly and serious.	(29)
8. Teachers in this school believe that their students have the ability to achieve academically.	(38)
*9. Academically oriented students in this school are ridiculed by their peers.	(44)

*Scored in reverse.

Scoring the OHI-M

Step 1: Score each item for each respondent with the appropriate number (1, 2, 3, or 4). Be sure to reverse score Items 7, 8, 13, 18, 23, 25, 26, 32, 37, 41, 44.

Step 2: Calculate an average school score for each item. In the example above, one would add all 50 scores on each item and then divide the sum by 50. Round the scores to the nearest hundredth. This score represents the average school item score. You should have 45 school item scores before proceeding.

Step 3: Sum the average school item scores as follows:

Institutional integrity (II) = 8 + 13 + 18 + 23 + 25 + 26 + 33
Collegial leadership (CL) = 1 + 4 + 5 + 10 + 14 + 24 + 30 + 35 + 39
Principal influence (PI) = 3 + 9 + 19 + 34 + 41 + 43
Resource support (RS) = 6 + 11 + 15 + 20 + 36 + 40
Teacher affiliation (TA) = 12 + 21 + 28 + 31 + 32 + 37 + 42 + 45
Academic emphasis (AE) = 2 + 7 + 16 + 17 + 22 + 27 + 29 + 38 + 44

These six scores represent the health profile of the school. You may wish to compare your school profile with other schools. To do so, we recommend that you standardize each school score. The current database on middle schools is drawn from a large, diverse sample of schools in New Jersey. The average scores and standard deviations for each health dimension are summarized as follows:

	Mean (M)	Standard Deviation (SD)
Institutional integrity (II)	16.41	2.82
Collegial leadership (CL)	26.61	3.71
Principal influence (PI)	16.37	2.12
Resource support (RS)	16.72	2.63
Teacher affiliation (TA)	28.34	2.57
Academic emphasis (AE)	20.11	2.80

Computing the Standardized Scores for the OHI-M

Step 1: Convert the school subtest scores to standardized scores with a mean of 500 and a standard deviation of 100, which we call SdS score. Use the following formulas:

SdS for II = 100(II − 16.41)/2.82 + 500

First compute the difference between your school score on II and the mean for the normative sample (II − 16.41). Then multiply the difference by one hundred [100(II − 16.41)]. Next divide

Table 3.3 Prototypic Profiles of Contrasting Health Types for Middle Schools

Health Dimension	Healthy School	Unhealthy School
Institutional integrity	553 (H)	443 (L)
Collegial leadership	634 (VH)	417 (L)
Principal influence	623 (VH)	398 (VL)
Resource support	580 (H)	414 (L)
Teacher affiliation	613 (VH)	411 (L)
Academic emphasis	617 (VH)	388 (VL)
Overall health	603 (VH)	412 (L)

VH = very high; H = high; L = low; VL = very low.

the product by the standard deviation of the normative sample (2.82). Then add 500 to the result. You have computed a standardized score (SdS) for the institutional integrity subscale.

Step 2: Repeat the process for each dimension as follows:

$$\text{SdS for CL} = 100(\text{CL} - 26.61)/3.71 + 500$$
$$\text{SdS for PI} = 100(\text{PI} - 16.37)/2.12 + 500$$
$$\text{SdS for RS} = 100(\text{RS} - 16.72)/2.63 + 500$$
$$\text{SdS for TA} = 100(\text{TA} - 28.34)/2.57 + 500$$
$$\text{SdS for AE} = 100(\text{AE} - 20.11)/2.80 + 500$$

You have standardized your school scores against the normative data provided in the New Jersey sample. For example, if your school score is 700 on institutional integrity, it is two standard deviations above the average score on institutional integrity of all schools in the sample; that is, the school has more institutional integrity than 97% of the schools in the sample.

An overall index of school health can be computed as follows:

$$\text{Health} = \frac{(\text{SdS for II}) + (\text{SdS for CL}) + (\text{SdS for PI}) + (\text{SdS for RS}) + (\text{SdS for TA}) + (\text{SdS for AE})}{6}$$

This health index is interpreted the same way as the subtest scores; that is, the mean of the "average" school is 500. Thus a score of 650 on the health index represents a very healthy school, one that is one and one half standard deviations above the average school. A score of 350 represents a school with a very sick climate. Most school scores, however, fall between these extremes and can only be diagnosed by carefully comparing all elements of the climate with the four prototypes.

Prototypic profiles for healthy and unhealthy schools have been constructed using the normative data from the New Jersey sample of middle schools (see Table 3.3). Here one can examine the fit of one's own school to the contrasting prototypes. An overall health index of 650 or more is almost certain to be the mark of a healthy school. We recommend using all six dimensions of OHI-M to gain a finely tuned picture of school health.

An Example

We assessed the climates of Wilson and Frost Middle Schools in the preceding chapter using the OCDQ-RM. We decided to look at their school climates through another lens, the health of the organization. To simplify our discussion, we often convert the number into categories ranging from high to low by using the following conversion table:

Above 600	Very high
551-600	High
525-550	Above average
511-524	Slightly above average
490-510	Average
476-489	Slightly below average
450-475	Below average
400-449	Low
Below 400	Very low

Let's revisit the climates of Wilson and Frost Middle Schools using the health measure from the OHI-M. Begin with Figure 3.1, which depicts the climate-health profile of Wilson.

Wilson Middle School is a healthy place to work and learn. Wilson is typical of schools in its relationship to the community. Parents place demands on the school, and most teachers don't like them, but the school has reasonable program integrity (average institutional integrity). The principal is a dynamic leader who is respected by teachers as well as superiors. The principal goes to bat for the teachers and is able to deliver for them (high principal influence). Teachers at Wilson get whatever resources they need to do the job; all they need do is ask (above average resource support). The principal is one of those gifted administrators who integrates a drive for the goals of the school with genuine support for teachers (very high collegial leadership). Teachers like Wilson. They identify with their school, are proud of their students, and respect each other (high teacher affiliation). Finally, the press for intellectual accomplishment is strong. Teachers set high expectations for their students, and students respond accordingly. The school is pervaded with a sense of purpose in learning (very high academic emphasis).

Frost, in contrast, is a sick middle school (see Figure 3.2). Not surprisingly, this closed climate (see Chapter 2) is an unhealthy school. The OHI-M, however, provides additional data and a different perspective of what is wrong with Frost than did the OCDQ-RM. Frost is a school in which outside groups demand change and more control over what goes on in

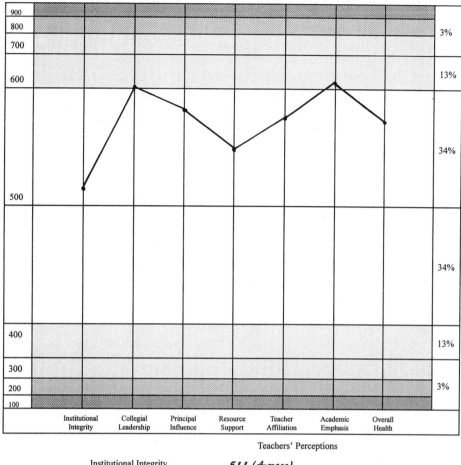

	Teachers' Perceptions
Institutional Integrity	*511 (Average)*
Collegial Leadership	*601 (Very High)*
Principal Influence	*583 (High)*
Resource Support	*546 (Above Average)*
Teacher Affiliation	*574 (High)*
Academic Emphasis	*612 (Very High)*
Overall Health	*571 (High)*

Figure 3.1. Organizational Health Inventory for Middle Schools (OHI-M): Wilson Middle School

school (very low institutional integrity). Instructional materials and supplies are difficult to obtain (low resource influence), and the principal has no apparent influence with either teachers (low collegial leadership) or

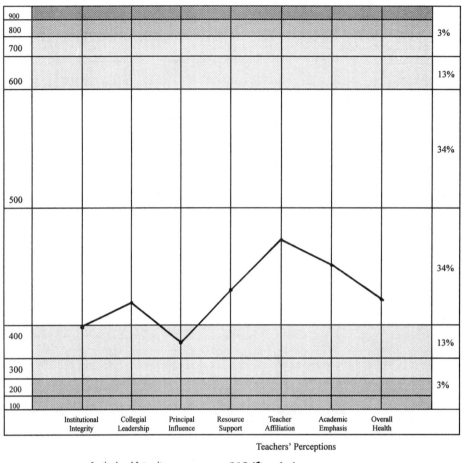

Teachers' Perceptions

Institutional Integrity	*398 (Very Low)*
Collegial Leadership	*415 (Low)*
Principal Influence	*350 (Very Low)*
Resource Support	*427 (Low)*
Teacher Affiliation	*472 (Slightly below average)*
Academic Emphasis	*450 (Low)*
Overall Health	*419 (Low)*

Figure 3.2. Organizational Health Inventory for Middle Schools (OHI-M): Frost Middle School

superiors, who ignore him (very low principal influence). There is a leadership vacuum. Teachers don't get along with each other and have limited attachment to the school and colleagues (slightly below average teacher affiliation). There are low expectations for student performance, and neither students nor teachers appreciate the hard work it takes to perform academically; teachers have no confidence in the students to achieve (low academic emphasis).

Conclusion

This chapter is a brief description of the OHI-M and how to administer and use it. Copy the instrument, administer it, and score it. For a clean copy of the OHI-M, see Appendix B. There is no copyright restriction for noncommercial use by schools; feel free to make as many copies as you wish. Then determine your school's climate profile and evaluate the health of the climate. Do you want to improve or change the climate? Before you engage in a school improvement plan, if you haven't already done so, we suggest that you assess the organizational climate of the school (Chapter 2). With both openness and health profiles in hand and knowledge of your own school, you are in a better position to plan change. Read Chapter 6 for some specific advice.

Note

1. Information on the reliability and validity of the OHI-M is reported in detail in Hoy, Barnes, and Sabo (1996) and Hoy and Sabo (in press).

4
Open Climates in Secondary Schools

A basic shortcoming of the original Organizational Climate Description Questionnaire (OCDQ) is that the instrument was developed for use in elementary schools. Secondary schools are more complicated than elementary schools; they have greater specialization, more division of labor, greater formalization, more rules and regulations, and more impersonality. In a word, they are more complex. Elementary and middle schools usually are feeder schools for the larger secondary schools, hence secondary schools are larger as well as more complex. It should come as no surprise to learn that an instrument designed to measure the climate of elementary schools is not satisfactory to assess the climate of high schools.

In the last chapter, we sketched the evolution of the OCDQ for middle schools. We now turn to the secondary school, a context wholly neglected by Halpin and Croft (1963) but addressed by Hoy, Tarter, and Kottkamp (1991) in an attempt to derive a climate measure specifically for the secondary school. The OCDQ-RS, the product of that research, is presented here to help principals use the work to improve the climate of their schools.

School Climate: A Personal View

School climate can be understood at two levels: a general and a specific one. Generally, school climate is the feeling that one experiences by walking around and spending some time in a school. Many people have commented that schools have a distinct feel or personality. They like the feeling in one school; they are uneasy in another. Halpin (1966) described the feel this way:

In one school the teachers and principals are zestful and ex-
ude confidence in what they are doing. They find pleasure working with each other. The pleasure is transmitted to students. . . .
In a second school the brooding discontent of the teachers is pal-
pable. The principal tries to hide his incompetence and his lack
of a sense of direction behind a cloak of authority. And yet, he
wears this cloak poorly because the attitude he displays to others
vacillates randomly between the obsequious and the officious.
And the psychology of sickness of such a faculty spills over on
the students who, in their own frustration, feed back to the teachers a mood of despair. A third school is marked by neither joy nor
despair, but by hollow ritual. Here one gets the feeling of watching an elaborate charade. . . . The acting is smooth, even glib, but
it appears to have little meaning for the participants; in a strange
way the show just doesn't seem to be "for real." (p. 131)

Hoy and his colleagues (1991) portrayed a substitute teacher's feel of a
new school as follows:

I used to give a good look at the physical condition of the
school and then the people inside the school. I was interested in
how they dressed, moved about the building, talked to each
other—those sorts of things. I got a preview of the people with
whom I would be working that day. These were of course impressions without ever talking to anybody in the school. My
guesses based on those impressions were often confirmed in my
first personal encounters. In some schools an administrator
greeted me and told we something about the assignment and the
school; in others a department chairperson. I knew I was in for a
hard day when "briefing the substitute" was left to a harried sec-
retary at the beginning of the school day.

Here and there I could see teachers talking with one another, having a last cup of coffee, or, as was the case in some
schools, simply isolated one from the other as little islands. Often
the good feelings teachers seemed to have for one another were
echoed in a pleasant classroom experience, but in those schools
where the teachers didn't seem to get along with one another, the
students were usually hellions. I knew the day would be a long
one and I was seldom disappointed. Graduate school taught me
conceptual labels for climate, but I had experienced it many
times without knowing its name. (p. 47)

These general feelings can be translated into a more systematic and
conceptual view of the feel of a school. Indeed, the atmosphere of a school
can be conceptualized and quantified in a reliable and valid way.

Rationale for the OCDQ-RS

Halpin and Croft's (1963) broad conception of open and closed climate remains conceptually meaningful. However, as we have noted in Chapter 1, the original *measure* of climate, the OCDQ—as opposed to the *conception* of open and closed climates—is dated, flawed, and one intended for elementary schools.

Principals are important in all schools. Yet secondary teachers are less likely to see the principal face to face on a daily basis than elementary teachers. Rather, they are more likely to work with assistant principals and department chairpersons. Secondary schools are staffed by teachers who consider themselves to be subject specialists and who are members of departments. Elementary schools, by way of comparison, generally are composed of teachers who are child-centered generalists concerned with total development of the child.

These difference were typically ignored by previous researchers (Carver & Sergiovanni, 1969; Kottkamp, Mulhern, & Hoy, 1987; Waldman, 1971). For these reasons and for the conceptual, psychometric, and methodological issues discussed in Chapter 1, we set about to measure the notion of climate as conceived by Halpin and Croft (1963) through an instrument formulated specifically for secondary schools.

The OCDQ for secondary schools examines the openness of teacher-teacher and teacher-principal interactions. In this chapter, we will briefly review the conceptual basis for the measure; then we will present the actual instrument and define its subscales; next we will describe the scoring procedures, norms, and interpretations. By the end of the chapter, you will have all the information that you need to administer, score, and interpret the scales.

Dimensions of the OCDQ-RS

The OCDQ-RS is a 34-item climate instrument with five dimensions describing the behavior of secondary teachers and principals. The instrument, unlike Halpin and Croft's (1963) original OCDQ, was designed for secondary schools. It measures two aspects of principal leadership: supportive and directive behavior. Supportive principal behavior meets both the social needs and task achievement of the faculty. The principal is helpful, genuinely concerned with teachers, and attempts to motivate them by using constructive criticism and by setting an example through hard work. In contrast, directive behavior is rigid and domineering control.

Similarly, three dimensions of teacher behavior are described—engaged, frustrated, and intimate. Engaged teacher behavior reflects a faculty in which teachers are proud of their school, enjoy working with each other, are supportive of their colleagues, and are committed to the success of their students. On the other hand, frustrated teacher behavior depicts a faculty burdened with routine duties, administrative paperwork, and excessive assignments unrelated to teaching. Finally, intimate teacher behavior reflects a strong and cohesive network of social relations among the faculty. The five basic dimensions of principal and teacher behavior are summarized as follows.

Principal's Behavior

Supportive principal behavior is characterized by efforts to motivate teachers by using constructive criticism and setting an example through hard work. At the same time, the principal is helpful and genuinely concerned with the personal and professional welfare of teachers. Supportive behavior is directed toward both the social needs and task achievement of the faculty.

Directive principal behavior is rigid and domineering supervision. The principal maintains close and constant control over all teachers and school activities down to the smallest details.

Teachers' Behavior

Engaged teacher behavior is reflected by high faculty morale. Teachers are proud of their school, enjoy working with each other, and are supportive of their colleagues. Teachers are not only concerned about each other, they are committed to the success of their students. They are friendly with students, trust students, and are optimistic about the ability of students to succeed.

Frustrated teacher behavior refers to a general pattern of interference from both administration and colleagues that distracts teachers from the basic task of teaching. Routine duties, administrative paperwork, and assigned nonteaching duties are excessive; moreover, teachers irritate, annoy, and interrupt each other.

Intimate teacher behavior reflects a strong and cohesive network of social relationships among the faculty. Teachers know each other well, are close personal friends, and regularly socialize together.

Additional Behavior Features

Four of the five aspects of school interaction also form a general dimension of school climate—openness.

Openness of the climate refers to a school climate where both the teachers' and principal's behaviors are authentic, energetic, goal directed, and supportive. Satisfaction is derived from both task accomplishment and social interaction. Open principal behavior is reflected in genuine relationships with teachers in which the principal creates a supportive environment, encourages teacher participation and contribution, and frees teachers from routine busywork so they can concentrate on teaching. In contrast, closed principal behavior is rigid, directive, and nonsupporitve. Open teacher behavior is characterized by sincere, positive, and supportive relationships with students, administrators, and colleagues; teachers are committed to their school and the success of their students; moreover, they find the work environment facilitating rather than frustrating.

Intimacy is a facet of secondary school climate that stands alone; unlike elementary and middle school climates, intimacy is not part of the openness construct. Intimate teacher behavior builds a strong and cohesive network of social relationships among the faculty. Teachers know each other well, have close personal friends among the faculty, and regularly socialize together. The friendly social interactions that are the essence of this construct are limited, however, to social needs; in fact, task accomplishment is not germane to this dimension.

Thus the OCDQ-RS provides a description of school climate in terms of five specific dimensions and a general openness dimension. Each school can be described by mapping its profile with these dimensions.

The OCDQ-RS Form

The OCDQ-RS is a 34-item questionnaire on which educators are asked to describe the extent to which specific behavior patterns occur in the school.[1] The responses vary along a 4-point scale defined by the categories *rarely occurs, sometimes occurs, often occurs,* and *very frequently occurs.* The entire instrument as it is administered to teachers is presented in Table 4.1.

Administering the Instrument

The OCDQ-RS is best administered as part of a faculty meeting. It is important to guarantee the anonymity of the teacher respondent; teachers are not asked to sign the questionnaire and no identifying code is placed on the form. Most teachers do not object to responding to the instrument, which takes less than 10 minutes to complete. It is probably advisable to have someone other than an administrator collect the data. It is important to create a nonthreatening atmosphere in which teachers give candid responses. All of the health and climate instruments follow the same pattern of administration.

The Subscales

After the 34-item instrument is administered, the specific items that provide the operational scales for each dimension are scored. The scales are presented in Table 4.2. Notice that the items are grouped by subtest, and in the right-hand column are the numbers that correspond to those on the instrument itself (Table 4.1).

Table 4.1 OCDQ-RS

Directions: The following are statements about your school. Please indicate the extent to which each statement characterizes your school by circling the appropriate response.

RO = rarely occurs; SO = sometimes occurs; O = often occurs; VFO = very frequently occurs

1. The mannerisms of teachers at this school are annoying.	RO SO O VFO
2. Teachers have too many committee requirements.	RO SO O VFO
3. Teachers spend time after school with students who have individual problems.	RO SO O VFO
4. Teachers are proud of their school.	RO SO O VFO
5. The principal sets an example by working hard himself or herself.	RO SO O VFO
6. The principal compliments teachers.	RO SO O VFO
7. Teacher-principal conferences are dominated by the principal.	RO SO O VFO
8. Routine duties interfere with the job of teaching.	RO SO O VFO
9. Teachers interrupt other faculty members who are talking in faculty meetings.	RO SO O VFO
10. Student government has an influence on school policy.	RO SO O VFO
11. Teachers are friendly with students.	RO SO O VFO
12. The principal rules with an iron fist.	RO SO O VFO
13. The principal monitors everything teachers do.	RO SO O VFO
14. Teachers' closest friends are other faculty members at this school.	RO SO O VFO
15. Administrative paperwork is burdensome at this school.	RO SO O VFO
16. Teachers help and support each other.	RO SO O VFO
17. Pupils solve their problems through logical reasoning.	RO SO O VFO
18. The principal closely checks teacher activities.	RO SO O VFO
19. The principal is autocratic.	RO SO O VFO
20. The morale of teachers is high.	RO SO O VFO
21. Teachers know the family background of other faculty members.	RO SO O VFO
22. Assigned nonteaching duties are excessive.	RO SO O VFO
23. The principal goes out of his or her way to help teachers.	RO SO O VFO
24. The principal explains his or her reason for criticism to teachers.	RO SO O VFO
25. The principal is available after school to help teachers when assistance is needed.	RO SO O VFO
26. Teachers invite other faculty members to visit them at home.	RO SO O VFO
27. Teachers socialize with each other on a regular basis.	RO SO O VFO
28. Teachers really enjoy working here.	RO SO O VFO
29. The principal uses constructive criticism.	RO SO O VFO
30. The principal looks out for the personal welfare of the faculty.	RO SO O VFO
31. The principal supervises teachers closely.	RO SO O VFO
32. The principal talks more than listens.	RO SO O VFO
33. Pupils are trusted to work together without supervision.	RO SO O VFO
34. Teachers respect the personal competence of their colleagues.	RO SO O VFO

SOURCE: John A. Mulhern, *The Organizational Climate of Secondary Schools: Revision of the OCDQ.* (Unpublished doctoral dissertation, Rutgers University, New Brunswick, New Jersey, 1984). Used with permission.

The items are scored by assigning 1 to *rarely occurs*, 2 to *sometimes occurs*, 3 to *often occurs*, and 4 to *very frequently occurs*. Each item is scored for each respondent, and then an average school score for *each item* is computed by

Table 4.2 Items That Compose the Five Subtests of the OCDQ-RS

Principal's behavior

Supportive behavior items	*Questionnaire no.*
1. The principal sets an example by working hard himself or herself.	(5)
2. The principal compliments teachers.	(6)
3. The principal goes out of his or her way to help teachers.	(23)
4. The principal explains his or her reasons for criticism to teachers.	(24)
5. The principal is available after school to help teachers when assistance is needed.	(25)
6. The principal uses constructive criticism.	(29)
7. The principal looks out for the personal welfare of the faculty.	(30)

Directive behavior items	*Questionnaire no.*
1. Teacher-principal conferences are dominated by the principal.	(7)
2. The principal rules with an iron fist.	(12)
3. The principal monitors everything teachers do.	(13)
4. The principal closely checks teacher activities.	(18)
5. The principal is autocratic.	(19)
6. The principal supervises teachers closely.	(31)
7. The principal talks more than listens.	(32)

Engaged behavior items	*Questionnaire no.*
1. Teachers spend time after school with students who have individual problems.	(3)
2. Teachers are proud of their school.	(4)
3. Student government has an influence on school policy.	(10)
4. Teachers are friendly with students.	(11)
5. Teachers help and support each other.	(16)
6. Pupils solve their problems through logical reasoning.	(17)
7. The morale of teachers is high.	(20)
8. Teachers really enjoy working here.	(28)
9. Pupils are trusted to work together without supervision.	(33)
10. Teachers respect the personal competence of their colleagues.	(34)

Frustrated behavior items	*Questionnaire no.*
1. The mannerisms of teachers at this school are annoying.	(1)
2. Teachers have too many committee requirements.	(2)
3. Routine duties interfere with the job of teaching.	(8)
4. Teachers interrupt other faculty members who are talking in faculty meetings.	(9)
5. Administrative paperwork is burdensome at this school.	(15)
6. Assigned nonteaching duties are excessive.	(22)

Table 4.2 Continued

Intimate behavior items	Questionnaire no.
1. Teachers' closest friends are other faculty members at this school.	(14)
2. Teachers know the family background of other faculty members.	(21)
3. Teachers invite other faculty members to visit them at home.	(26)
4. Teachers socialize with each other on a regular basis.	(27)

averaging the item responses across the school; remember, the school is the unit of analysis. For example, if School A has 56 teachers responding to the OCDQ-RS, each individual questionnaire is scored and then an average score for all respondents is computed for each item. Thus the average score for the 56 teachers is calculated for Item 1, then Item 2, and so on. The average school scores for the items comprising each subtest are added to yield school subtest scores. The five subtest scores represent the climate profile for the school.

Scoring the OCDQ-RS

Step 1: Score each item for each respondent with the appropriate number (1, 2, 3, or 4).

Step 2: Calculate an average school score for each item. Round the scores to the nearest hundredth. This score represents the average school item score. You should have 34 average school item scores before proceeding.

Step 3: Sum the average school item scores as follows:

Supportive behavior (S) = 5 + 6 + 23 + 24 + 25 + 29 + 30
Directive behavior (D) = 7 + 12 + 13 + 18 + 19 + 31 + 32
Engaged behavior (E) = 3 + 4 + 10 + 11 + 16 + 17 + 20 + 28 + 33 + 34
Frustrated behavior (F) = 1 + 2 + 8 + 9 + 15 + 22
Intimate behavior (Int) = 14 + 21 + 26 + 27

You may wish to compare your school's profile with other schools. We recommend that you convert each school score to a standardized score. The current database on secondary schools is drawn from a large, diverse sample of schools from New Jersey. The average scores and standard deviations for each climate dimension are as follows:

	Mean (M)	*Standard Deviation (SD)*
Supportive behavior (S)	18.19	2.66
Directive behavior (D)	13.96	2.49
Engaged behavior (E)	26.45	1.32
Frustrated behavior (F)	12.33	1.98
Intimate behavior (Int)	8.80	0.92

Computing Standardized Score of the OCDQ-RS

Step 1: Convert the school subtest scores to standardized scores with a mean of 500 and a standard deviation of 100, which we call SdS scores. Use the following formulas:

$$\text{SdS for } S = 100(S - 18.19)/2.66 + 500$$

> First compute the difference between your school score on S and the mean for the normative sample (S – 18.19). Then multiply the difference by one hundred [100(S – 18.19)]. Next divide the product by the standard deviation of the normative sample (2.66). Then add 500 to the result. You have computed a standardized score (SdS) for the supportive behavior subscale (S).

Step 2: Repeat the process for each dimension as follows:

$$\text{SdS for } D = 100(D - 13.96)/2.49 + 500$$
$$\text{SdS for } E = 100(E - 26.45)/1.32 + 500$$
$$\text{SdS for } F = 100(F - 12.33)/1.98 + 500$$
$$\text{SdS for } Int = 100(Int - 8.80)/0.92 + 500$$

You have standardized your school scores against the normative data provided in the New Jersey sample. For example, if your school score is 600 on supportive behavior, it is one standard deviation above the average score on supportive behavior of all schools in the sample; that is, the principal is more supportive than 84% of the other principals. A score of 300 represents a school that is two standard deviations below the mean on the subtest. You may recognize this system as the one used in reporting individual scores on the SAT, CEEB, and GRE.

There is one other score that can be easily computed and is often of interest: the general openness index for the school climate.

$$\text{Openness} = \frac{(\text{SdS for } S) + (1000 - \text{SdS for } D) + (\text{SdS for } E) + (1000 - \text{SdS for } F)}{4}$$

This openness index is interpreted the same way as the subtest scores; that is, the mean of the "average" school is 500. Thus a score of 600 on

Table 4.3 Prototypic Profiles of Open and Closed Secondary School Climate

Climate Dimension	Open Climate	Closed Climate
Supportive	629 (VH)	398 (VL)
Directive	414 (L)	642 (VH)
Engaged	627 (VH)	383 (VL)
Frustrated	346 (VL)	641 (VH)
Intimate	465 (L)	463 (L)
School openness	624 (VH)	375 (VL)

VH = very high; H = high; L = low; VL = very low.

openness represents a highly open school climate, one that is one standard deviation above the average school; this means that the school is more open than 84% of the schools in the normative sample.

Prototypic profiles for the climate of schools have been constructed using the normative data from the New Jersey sample of secondary schools (see Table 4.3). Thus one can examine the fit of one's own school to the contrasting prototypes. An overall openness score of 620 or more, for instance, is almost certain to be the mark of an open school. We recommend, however, using all five dimensions of OCDQ-RS to gain a finely tuned picture of school climate.

An Example

The climate-openness profiles for two high schools, McKinley and Harding, and a brief sketch of the climate of each school are included in this section. We were invited to survey McKinley High School in a school district proud of its tradition of quality. The motto of the district is "In Search of Excellence." The climate profile at McKinley and a brief sketch of its meaning follow.

To help in the discussion of school climate profiles, we sometimes change the numbers into categories ranging from high to low by using the following conversion table:

Above 600	Very high
551-600	High
525-550	Above average
511-524	Slightly above average
490-510	Average
476-489	Slightly below average
450-475	Below average
400-449	Low
Below 400	Very low

School data can be scored by hand or by our computer program, which includes a comparison of your school with the normative sample and classifies the climate.[2]

We begin with a climate profile for McKinley (see Figure 4.1). The five subtest scores and school openness scores were computed using the formulas to standardize the scores just described.

Students and faculty like being at McKinley. Teachers find that the principal arrives earlier than most of them and stays a bit later; they can rely on the principal to help them and to be a constructive force in the improvement of instruction (very high supportive behavior). Teachers feel that they work with a principal who listens more than talks, respects their autonomy as professionals, and is a source of sound advice (low directive behavior). The teachers are proud to be a part of McKinley and enjoy their work with students who, in turn, are responsible influences on school life (high engaged behavior). Committee work at McKinley is limited, purposeful, and does not interfere with teaching responsibilities (very low frustrated behavior). The teachers often entertain one another in their homes as their friendships at school flow into their personal lives outside of school (above average intimacy). Even casual visitors to the school are impressed by the friendliness and openness of the professional staff, an observation strongly supported by the results of the OCDQ-RS. Clearly, McKinley High School has a positive and open organizational climate (see Figure 4.1)

We were not invited to assess Harding High School and probably with good reason. It is, however, an actual school from our data set. We scored the school following the instructions provided earlier in the chapter. The climate-openness profile at Harding and a vignette of its climate follow (see Figure 4.2).

Harding High School has a closed organizational climate. Here is a principal who is trying hard but to little avail. He sets an example of commitment and industriousness for his teachers. At the same time, he shows concern and support for his faculty and asks them to do nothing that he is not already doing (above average support). But as much as he is concerned about the welfare of the teachers, he does not give them the freedom to act on their own initiative; he is directive (high). Teacher behavior at Harding is about as closed as you will find in any high school. Morale is extremely low. Teachers don't like each other, the school, or the students (very low engagement). They are frustrated by the close monitoring of the administration and what they consider to be excessive paperwork and meaningless routine (very high frustration). There is no cohesiveness among the faculty in this school (low intimacy); they neither work together nor socialize together.

We cannot comment on why the school has this pattern because we have no data other than this snapshot of the school. The climate profile is the beginning of a process of diagnosis and eventual change, not an end in itself. We received no invitation to suggest strategies for Harding High. Until the administration and teachers decide that they want to change, we

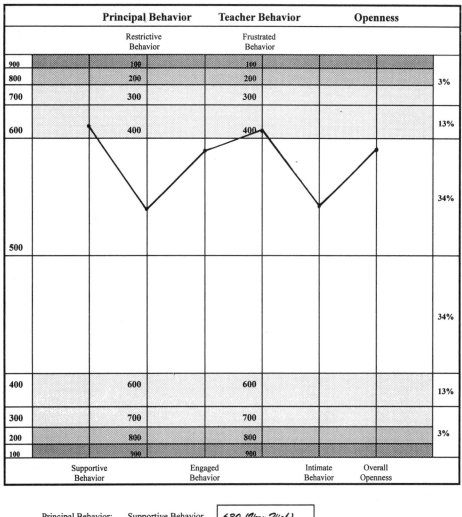

	Principal Behavior	Teacher Behavior	Openness
	Restrictive Behavior	Frustrated Behavior	

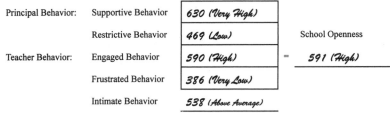

Principal Behavior:	Supportive Behavior	630 (Very High)	
	Restrictive Behavior	469 (Low)	School Openness
Teacher Behavior:	Engaged Behavior	590 (High)	= 591 (High)
	Frustrated Behavior	386 (Very Low)	
	Intimate Behavior	538 (Above Average)	

Figure 4.1. Organizational Climate Description Questionnaire for Secondary Schools (OCDQ-RS): McKinley High School

suspect that the school will muddle through with teachers and administrators playing games with each other. All participants are frustrated, and the students are the ultimate losers—not a good place to work, not a good place to learn.

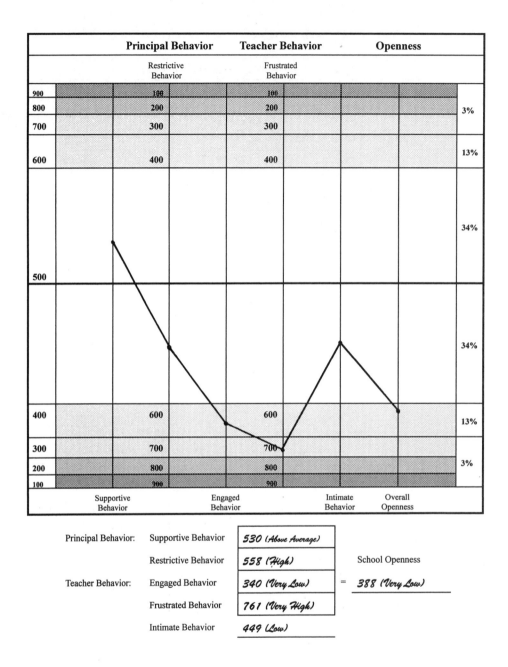

Figure 4.2. Organizational Climate Description Questionnaire for Secondary Schools (OCDQ-RS): Harding High School

Similarly, we cannot account for the open pattern at McKinley. We can only say that any educational innovation will likely be successful in an atmosphere that is supportive and manifestly dedicated to professional development. McKinley is a school where good things happen because the basic dynamics of personal and professional interaction are so favorable to constructive change.

Conclusion

This chapter is a lean description of the OCDQ-RS and how to administer and use it. Copy the instrument, administer it, and score it. For a clean copy of the OCDQ-RS, see Appendix C. There is no copyright restriction for noncommercial use by schools; feel free to make as many copies as you wish. Then determine your school's climate profile and evaluate the openness of the climate. Do you want to improve or change the climate? Before you engage in a school improvement plan, we suggest you assess the organizational health of the school (Chapter 5). If the school faculty is relatively large, we suggest that you administer both the OCDQ-RS and the OHI-S at the same meeting, distributing the two instruments randomly. With both openness and health profiles in hand and knowledge of your own school, you are in a better position to plan change. Read Chapter 6 for some specific advice.

Notes

1. Information on the reliability and validity of the OCDQ-RS and the OHI-S (discussed in Chapter 5) is reported in detail in Hoy, Tarter, and Kottkamp (1991).

2. Computer scoring programs for both the OCDQ-RS and the OHI-S are available from Arlington Writers, 2548 Onandaga Drive, Columbus, Ohio 43221. The programs, which run on Windows 3.1 or later versions, will score each subtest, standardize school scores, and provide indexes of openness and health. Further information on the scoring program can be obtained from Arlington Writers (fax 614-488-5075) or see Appendix E.

5
Healthy Climates in Secondary Schools

The Organizational Health Inventory (OHI) is another instrument to assess the climate of schools. The inventory in this chapter was especially developed and tested for secondary schools (OHI-S); it describes the health of interpersonal relations in schools among students, teachers, administrators, and community members. In the following pages, we will briefly sketch the conceptual foundations of the OHI-S, provide the actual questionnaire for use in schools, specify the scoring procedures, and discuss the analysis and interpretation of the results.

OHI for Secondary Schools: OHI-S

A healthy school is one in which the institutional, administrative, and teacher levels are in harmony, and the school meets functional needs as it successfully copes with disruptive external forces and directs its energies toward its mission. Health is conceptualized at three levels: institutional, administrative, and teacher. Dimensions of health were selected to represent the basic needs of schools: to adapt to environmental demands, achieve goals, satisfy participant needs, and create a cohesive community.

The *institutional level* connects the school with its environment. Schools need legitimacy and support from the community. A dimension called institutional integrity was conceived as the ability of the school to remain relatively independent from vested interests. Both administrators and teachers need backing to perform their functions relatively unfettered by individuals and groups outside the school.

The *administrative level* controls the internal managerial function of the organization. Principals are the administrative officers of the school. They allocate resources and coordinate the work effort. They must find ways to develop teacher loyalty, trust, and commitment as well as to motivate teachers and to influence their own superiors. Consideration and initiating structure combine social support of teachers with the organization of work to accomplish school goals. Principal influence and resource support are basic leadership activities that ensure the presence of adequate instructional materials and resources requested by teachers.

The *teacher level* of the school is concerned with the teaching-learning process. The primary function of the school is to produce educated students. Moreover, teachers and supervisors have immediate responsibility for solving the problems associated with effective learning and teaching. Morale, a key mechanism for integrating school life, builds a cohesive work unit. Academic emphasis, the school's press for achievement, is the setting of high but achievable student goals and the commitment of both students and teachers to academic excellence. These fundamental features of school health are summarized as follows.

Institutional Level

Institutional integrity describes a school that has integrity in its educational program. The school is not vulnerable to narrow, vested interests of community groups; indeed, teachers are protected from unreasonable community and parental demands. The school is able to cope successfully with destructive outside forces.

Administrative Level

Initiating structure is task- and achievement-oriented behavior. The principal makes his or her attitudes and expectations clear to the faculty and maintains definite standards of performance.

Consideration is principal behavior that is friendly, supportive, and collegial. The principal looks out for the welfare of faculty members and is open to their suggestions.

Principal influence is the principal's ability to influence the actions of superiors. The influential principal is persuasive, works effectively with the superintendent, and simultaneously demonstrates independence in thought and action.

Resource support refers to a school where adequate classroom and instructional materials are available and extra materials are easily obtained.

Teacher Level

Morale is the sense of trust, confidence, enthusiasm, and friendliness among teachers. Teachers feel good about each other and, at the same time, feel a sense of accomplishment from their jobs.

Academic emphasis refers to the school's press for achievement. High but achievable goals are set for students, the learning environment is orderly and serious, teachers believe students can achieve, and students work hard and respect those who do well academically.

A healthy school is one in which the teacher, administrative, and institutional levels are in harmony. The school meets its needs of adaptation, goal achievement, participant satisfaction, and group cohesiveness as it successfully copes with disruptive external forces and directs its energies toward its mission. School health captures the positive contribution of all seven dimensions. Brief vignettes of the healthy and sick school are now described.

Healthy School

A healthy school is protected from unreasonable community and parental pressures. The board successfully resists all narrow efforts of vested interest groups to influence policy (high institutional integrity). The principal of a healthy school is a dynamic leader, integrating both task-oriented and relations-oriented leader behavior. Such behavior is supportive of teachers and yet provides high standards for performance (high consideration and initiating structure). Moreover, the principal has influence with his or her superiors, which is demonstrated by the ability to get what is needed for the effective operation of the school (high influence). Teachers in a healthy school are committed to teaching and learning. They set high but achievable goals for their students, maintain high standards of performance, and promote a serious and orderly learning environment. Furthermore, students work hard on their schoolwork, are highly motivated, and respect other students who achieve academically (high academic emphasis). Classroom supplies, instructional materials, and supplementary materials are always available (high resource support). Finally, teachers like each other, trust each other, are enthusiastic about their work, and identify with the school. They are proud of their school (high morale).

Sick School

A sick school is vulnerable to destructive outside forces. Teachers and administrators are bombarded by unreasonable parental demands, and the school is buffeted by the whims of the public (low institutional integrity). The school is without leadership. The principal provides little direction or structure (low initiating structure), exhibits little encouragement and support for teachers (low consideration), and has little clout with superiors (low influence). Teachers don't feel good about their colleagues or their jobs. They act aloof, suspicious, and defensive (low morale). Instructional materials, supplies, and supplementary materials are not available when needed (low resource support). Finally, there is little press for academic excellence. Apathy is pervasive. Neither teachers nor students take academic life seriously; in fact, academically oriented students are ridiculed by their peers and viewed by their teachers as threats (low academic emphasis).

The OHI-S Form

The OHI-S is a 44-item questionnaire on which educators are asked to describe the extent to which specific behavior patterns occur in the school. The responses vary along a 4-point scale defined by the categories *rarely occurs, sometimes occurs, often occurs,* and *very frequently occurs.* The entire instrument as it is administered to teachers is presented in Table 5.1.

Administering the Instrument

The OHI-S is best administered as part of a faculty meeting. It is important to guarantee the anonymity of the teacher respondent; teachers are not asked to sign the questionnaire and no identifying code is placed on the form. Most teachers do not object to responding to the instrument, which takes less than 10 minutes to complete. We recommend that someone other than an administrator collect the data. It is important to create a nonthreatening atmosphere in which teachers give candid responses. All of the health instruments follow the same pattern of administration.

The Subscales

After the 44-item instrument is administered to the faculty, the items for each scale are scored. The items for each scale are presented in Table 5.2.

The items are scored by assigning 1 to *rarely occurs,* 2 to *sometimes occurs,* 3 to *often occurs,* and 4 to *very frequently occurs.* When an item is reversed scored (noted by an asterisk in Table 5.2), *rarely occurs* receives a 4, *sometimes occurs* a 3, and so on. Each item is scored for the each respondent, and then an average school score for *each item* is computed by averaging the item responses across the school; remember, the school is the unit of analysis. The average school scores for the items comprising each subtest are added to yield school subtest scores. The seven subtest scores represent the health profile for the school. For example, if School A has 60 teachers responding to the OHI-S, each individual questionnaire is scored and then an average score for all respondents is computed for each item. Thus the average score for the 60 teachers is calculated for Item 1, then Item 2, and so on. The average school scores for the items defining each subtest are added to yield school subtest scores. The seven subtest scores represent the health profile for the school.

Table 5.1 OHI-S

Directions: The following are statements about your school. Please indicate the extent to which each statement characterizes your school by circling the appropriate response.

RO = rarely occurs; SO = sometimes occurs; O = often occurs; VFO = very frequently occurs

1. Teachers are protected from unreasonable community and parental demands.	RO SO O VFO
2. The principal gets what he or she asks for from superiors.	RO SO O VFO
3. The principal is friendly and approachable.	RO SO O VFO
4. The principal asks that faculty members follow standard rules and regulations.	RO SO O VFO
5. Extra materials are available if requested.	RO SO O VFO
6. Teachers do favors for each other.	RO SO O VFO
7. Students in this school can achieve the goals that have been set for them.	RO SO O VFO
8. The school is vulnerable to outside pressures.	RO SO O VFO
9. The principal is able to influence the actions of his or her superiors.	RO SO O VFO
10. The principal treats all faculty members as his or her equal.	RO SO O VFO
11. The principal makes his or her attitudes clear to the school.	RO SO O VFO
12. Teachers are provided with adequate materials for their classrooms.	RO SO O VFO
13. Teachers in this school like each other.	RO SO O VFO
14. The school sets high standards for academic performance.	RO SO O VFO
15. Community demands are accepted even when they are not consistent with the educational program.	RO SO O VFO
16. The principal is able to work well with the superintendent.	RO SO O VFO
17. The principal puts suggestions made by the faculty into operation.	RO SO O VFO
18. The principal lets faculty know what is expected of them.	RO SO O VFO
19. Teachers receive necessary classroom supplies.	RO SO O VFO
20. Teachers are indifferent to each other.	RO SO O VFO
21. Students respect others who get good grades.	RO SO O VFO
22. Teachers feel pressure from the community.	RO SO O VFO
23. The principal's recommendations are given serious consideration by his or her superiors.	RO SO O VFO
24. The principal is willing to make changes.	RO SO O VFO
25. The principal maintains definite standards of performance.	RO SO O VFO
26. Supplementary materials are available for classroom use.	RO SO O VFO
27. Teachers exhibit friendliness to each other.	RO SO O VFO
28. Students seek extra work so they can get good grades.	RO SO O VFO
29. Select citizen groups are influential with the board.	RO SO O VFO
30. The principal is impeded by superiors.	RO SO O VFO
31. The principal looks out for the personal welfare of faculty members.	RO SO O VFO
32. The principal schedules the work to be done.	RO SO O VFO
33. Teachers have access to needed instructional materials.	RO SO O VFO
34. Teachers in this school are cool and aloof to each other.	RO SO O VFO
35. Teachers in this school believe that their students have the ability to achieve academically.	RO SO O VFO
36. The school is open to the whims of the public.	RO SO O VFO
37. The morale of teachers is high.	RO SO O VFO
38. Academic achievement is recognized and acknowledged by the school.	RO SO O VFO
39. A few vocal parents can change school policy.	RO SO O VFO
40. There is a feeling of trust and confidence among the staff.	RO SO O VFO
41. Students try hard to improve on previous work.	RO SO O VFO

Table 5.1 Continued

42. Teachers accomplish their jobs with enthusiasm.	RO SO O VFO
43. The learning environment is orderly and serious.	RO SO O VFO
44. Teachers identify with the school.	RO SO O VFO

SOURCE: John Feldman, *The School Health Index: The Development and Test of an Instrument Using a Parsonian and Etzonian Perspective.* (Unpublished doctoral dissertation, Rutgers University, New Brunswick, New Jersey, 1985.) Used with permission.

Table 5.2 Items That Compose the Seven Subtests of the OHI-S

Institutional level

Institutional integrity items	*Questionnaire no.*
1. Teachers are protected from unreasonable community and parental demands.	(1)
*2. The school is vulnerable to outside pressures.	(8)
*3. Community demands are accepted even when they are not consistent with the educational program.	(15)
*4. Teachers feel pressure from the community.	(22)
*5. Select citizen groups are influential with the board.	(29)
*6. The school is open to the whims of the public.	(36)
*7. A few vocal parents can change school policy.	(39)

Administrative level

Initiating structure items	*Questionnaire no.*
1. The principal asks that faculty members follow standard rules and regulations.	(4)
2. The principal makes his or her attitudes clear to the school.	(11)
3. The principal lets faculty know what is expected of them.	(18)
4. The principal maintains definite standards of performance.	(25)
5. The principal schedules the work to be done.	(32)

Consideration items	*Questionnaire no.*
1. The principal is friendly and approachable.	(3)
2. The principal treats all faculty members as his or her equal.	(10)
3. The principal puts suggestions made by the faculty into operation.	(17)
4. The principal is willing to make changes.	(24)
5. The principal looks out for the personal welfare of faculty members.	(31)

Principal influence items	*Questionnaire no.*
1. The principal gets what he or she asks for from superiors.	(2)
2. The principal is able to influence the actions of his or her superiors.	(9)
3. The principal is able to work well with the superintendent.	(16)
4. The principal's recommendations are given serious consideration by his or her superiors.	(23)
*5. The principal is impeded by superiors.	(30)

(continued on the next page)

Table 5.2 Continued

Resource support items	*Questionnaire no.*
1. Extra materials are available if requested.	(5)
2. Teachers are provided with adequate materials for their classrooms.	(12)
3. Teachers receive necessary classroom supplies.	(19)
4. Supplementary materials are available for classroom use.	(26)
5. Teachers have access to instructional material.	(33)

Morale items	*Questionnaire no.*
1. Teachers do favors for each other.	(6)
2. Teachers in this school like each other.	(13)
*3. Teachers are indifferent to each other.	(20)
4. Teachers exhibit friendliness to each other.	(27)
*5. Teachers in this school are cool and aloof to each other.	(34)
6. The morale of teachers is high.	(37)
7. There is a feeling of trust and confidence among the staff.	(40)
8. Teachers accomplish their jobs with enthusiasm.	(42)
9. Teachers identify with the school.	(44)

Academic emphasis items	*Questionnaire no.*
1. Students in this school can achieve the goals that have been set for them.	(7)
2. The school sets high standards for academic perfomance.	(14)
3. Students respect others who get good grades.	(21)
4. Students seek extra work so they can get good grades.	(28)
5. Teachers in this school believe that their students have the ability to achieve academically.	(35)
6. Academic achievement is recognized and acknowledged by the school.	(38)
7. Students try hard to improve on previous work.	(41)
8. The learning environment is orderly and serious.	(43)

*Scored in reverse.

Scoring the OHI-S

Step 1: Score each item for each respondent with the appropriate number (1, 2, 3, or 4). Be sure to reverse score items 8, 15, 20, 22, 29, 30, 34, 36, and 39.

Step 2: Calculate an average school score for each item. In the example above, one would add all 60 scores on each item and then divide the sum by 60. Round the scores to the nearest hundredth. This score represents the average school item score. You should have 44 school item scores before proceeding.

Step 3: Sum the average school item scores as follows:

> Institutional integrity (II) = 1 + 8 + 15 + 22 + 29 + 36 + 39
> Initiating structure (IS) = 4 + 11 + 18 + 25 + 32
> Consideration (C) = 3 + 10 + 17 + 24 + 31
> Principal influence (PI) = 2 + 9 + 16 + 23 + 30
> Resource support (RS) = 5 + 12 + 19 + 26 + 33
> Morale (M) = 6 + 13 + 20 + 27 + 34 + 37 + 40 + 42 + 44
> Academic emphasis (AE) = 7 + 14 + 21 + 28 + 35 + 38 + 41 + 43

These seven scores represent the health profile of the school. You may wish to compare your school profile with other schools. To do so, we recommend that you standardize each school score. The current database on secondary schools is drawn from a large, diverse sample of schools from New Jersey. The average scores and standard deviations for each health dimension are summarized below:

	Mean (M)	*Standard Deviation (SD)*
Institutional integrity (II)	18.61	2.66
Initiating structure (IS)	14.36	1.83
Consideration (C)	12.83	2.03
Principal influence (PI)	12.93	1.79
Resource support (RS)	13.52	1.89
Morale (M)	25.05	2.64
Academic emphasis (AE)	21.33	2.76

Computing the Standardized Scores for the OHI-S

Step 1: Convert the school subtest scores to standardized scores with a mean of 500 and a standard deviation of 100, which we call SdS score. Use the following formulas:

SdS for II = 100(II − 18.61)/2.66 + 500

> First compute the difference between your school score on II and the mean for the normative sample (II − 18.61). Then multiply the difference by one hundred [100(II − 18.61)]. Next divide the product by the standard deviation of the normative sample (2.66). Then add 500 to the result. You have computed a standardized score (SdS) for the institutional integrity subscale.

Step 2: Repeat the process for each dimension as follows:

> SdS for IS = 100(IS − 14.36)/1.83 + 500
> SdS for C = 100(C − 12.83)/2.03 + 500

Table 5.3 Prototypic Profiles of Contrasting Health Types for Secondary Schools

Health Dimension	Healthy School	Unhealthy School
Institutional integrity	605 (VH)	443 (L)
Initiating structure	659 (VH)	404 (L)
Consideration	604 (VH)	390 (VL)
Principal influence	634 (VH)	360 (VL)
Resource support	598 (H)	404 (L)
Morale	603 (VH)	402 (L)
Academic emphasis	603 (VH)	383 (VL)
Overall health	615 (VH)	398 (VL)

VH = very high; H = high; L = low; VL = very low.

$$\text{SdS for PI} = 100(\text{PI} - 12.93/1.79 + 500$$
$$\text{SdS for RS} = 100(\text{RS} - 13.52)/1.89 + 500$$
$$\text{SdS for M} = 100(\text{M} - 25.05)/2.64 + 500$$
$$\text{SdS for AE} = 100(\text{AE} - 21.33)/2.76 + 500$$

You have standardized your school scores against the normative data provided in the New Jersey sample. For example, if your school score is 700 on institutional integrity, it is two standard deviations above the average score on institutional integrity of all schools in the sample; that is, the school has more institutional integrity than 97% of the schools in the sample.

An overall index of school health can be computed as follows:

$$\text{Health} = \frac{(\text{SdS for II}) + (\text{SdS for IS}) + (\text{SdS for C}) + (\text{SdS for PI}) + (\text{SdS for RS}) + (\text{SdS for M}) + (\text{SdS for AE})}{7}$$

This health index is interpreted the same way as the subtest scores; that is, the mean of the "average" school is 500. Thus a score of 650 on the health index represents a very healthy school, one that is one and one half standard deviations above the average school, and a score of 400 represents a very sick school climate. Most school scores, however, fall between these extremes and can only be diagnosed by carefully comparing all elements of the climate.

Prototypic profiles for healthy and unhealthy schools have been constructed using the normative data from the New Jersey sample of secondary schools (see Table 5.3). Here one can examine the fit of one's own school to the contrasting prototypes. An overall health index of 600 or more is almost certain to be the mark of a healthy school. We recommend using all seven dimensions of the OHI-S to gain a finely tuned picture of school health.

An Example

We assessed the openness of the climate of Harding High School in the preceding chapter, using the OCDQ-RS. We decided to look at Harding High from another vantage point, the health of the school climate (see Figure 5.1). To simplify our discussion, remember that we often convert the number into categories ranging from high to low by using the following conversion table:

Above 600	Very high
551-600	High
525-550	Above average
511-524	Slightly above average
490-510	Average
476-489	Slightly below average
450-475	Below average
400-449	Low
Below 400	Very low

Harding is a sick school. This is a real school; only the name has been changed. Not surprisingly, its closed climate (see Chapter 4) shows that it is an unhealthy school. The OHI-S, however, provides additional data and a different perspective of what is wrong with Harding than did the OCDQ-RS. Harding is a school in which outside groups are attempting to influence educational decisions within the school (low institutional integrity). Instructional materials and supplies are difficult to obtain (very low resource support), and the principal, although seen as friendly, supportive, and collegial (average consideration), has no apparent influence with superiors, who do not take him seriously (very low principal influence). The principal's attempts to maintain structure within the school are below the average of other high schools. Teachers do not get much of a sense of accomplishment from their jobs nor are they confident in their fellow teachers or even friendly with them (very low morale). The press for academic achievement in Harding is abysmal; teachers have no confidence in the students to achieve.

These new data about Harding supply hints about its problems. This may well be a school that is being starved. The principal seems to be in an untenable position. He is reasonably well liked by the teachers, but he has no influence with his superiors in the central administration. He has been unable to get what the teachers feel are the necessary instructional materials to do a good job. His faculty is apathetic and demoralized; in fact, it seems as though they have given up. The problems of Harding may not be merely school problems; they appear to be part of a district pattern of neglect.

It would be tempting to suggest changes that ought to be made at Harding, but it would probably not be productive. The teachers and

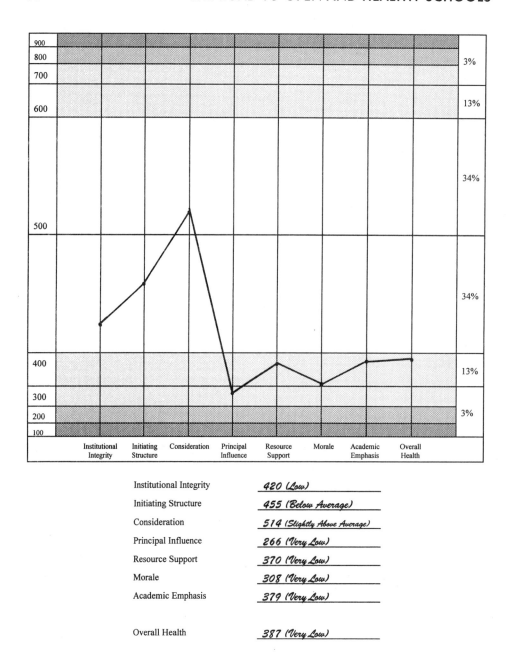

Figure 5.1. Organizational Health Inventory for Secondary Schools (OHI-S): Harding High School

administrators at Harding are the best people to explain why this pattern of unhealthy dynamics exists. And they are critically placed to suggest and implement possibilities for change. Any program of successful change must involve the teachers at Harding. Climate and health profiles are only means toward effective change, not ends in themselves.

It is also instructive to examine the organizational health of McKinley High School, which has an open organizational climate (see Chapter 4). Thus we turn to Figure 5.2 and examine the health profile of McKinley.

McKinley High School is a healthy school. The principal's leadership is strong. She provides direction by initiating structure to solve problems and accomplish tasks (high initiating structure), but she is constructive and supportive in her relations with teachers (very high consideration). She respects the professionalism of her teachers and is successful in persuading the superintendent of the quality of her staff (high principal influence); consequently, she has no difficulty getting extra resources as they are needed by her faculty (very high resource support). However, the most compelling aspect of McKinley is its press for high academic achievement (very high academic emphasis). As one might expect at a school that is ably led and unusually effective with its students, the teachers are committed to the school, their colleagues, and the students (high morale). It is also not surprising that this school had one of the highest achievement rates for students in the state.

Conclusion

This chapter is a description of the OHI-S and how to administer and use it. Copy the instrument, administer it, and score it. For a clean copy of the OHI-S, see Appendix D. There is no copyright restriction for noncommercial use by schools; feel free to make as many copies as you wish. Then determine your school's climate profile and evaluate the health of the climate. Do you want to improve or change the climate? Before you engage in a school improvement plan, if you haven't already done so, we suggest that you assess the organizational climate of the school (Chapter 4). The easiest way to collect both health and openness data on the climate of you school is to distribute both the OHI-S and the OCDQ-RS at a faculty meeting. At random, half the faculty should be given one instrument and the other half should be given the other instrument. With both openness and health profiles in hand and knowledge of your own school, you are in a better position to plan change. Read Chapter 6 for some specific advice.

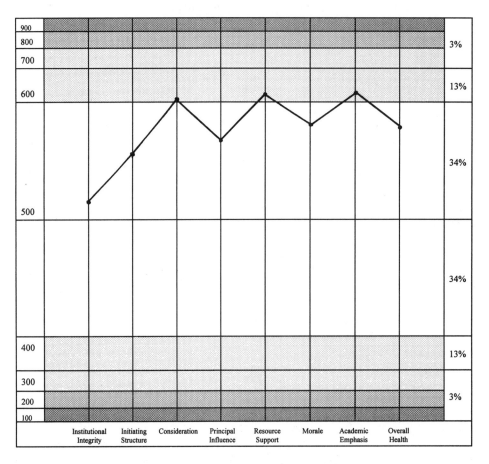

	Institutional Integrity	Initiating Structure	Consideration	Principal Influence	Resource Support	Morale	Academic Emphasis	Overall Health	
900									
800									3%
700									
600									13%
500									34%
									34%
400									13%
300									
200									3%
100									

Institutional Integrity	*511 (Slightly Above Avg)*
Initiating Structure	*553 (High)*
Consideration	*603 (Very High)*
Principal Influence	*558 (High)*
Resource Support	*615 (Very High)*
Morale	*583 (High)*
Academic Emphasis	*621 (Very High)*
Overall Health	*578 (High)*

Figure 5.2. Organizational Health Inventory for Secondary Schools (OHI-S): McKinley High School

6

Improving School Climate

You now have the tools to map the climate of your school. Having done so, what's next? It depends on what you find and where you want to go. Problems are discrepancies between what you have and what you want. You have a problem if there is a discrepancy between the profile of climate scores of the principal and those of the teachers. You also have a problem if there is a discrepancy between the actual school scores and what is expected. Ordinarily, you have a problem if the discrepancy puts your school below the scores of the typical healthy school in the normative sample; that is, most educators want to have an average or better school, and the prototypic profiles tell you where your school stands. Remember, a score of less than 500 puts you below the average school. In brief, there are two typical discrepancy problems regarding school climate:

- Discrepancy between the principal's and teachers' perceptions
- Discrepancy between the actual and desired profile of school climate

The challenge to change is formidable, but it is manageable and attainable. We hope to allay your qualms by providing you with actual examples.

Sandburg Middle School: Discrepancy Between Principal's and Teachers' Perceptions

Sandburg Middle School distinguishes itself comfortably from other suburban middle schools. It is conspicuous in its consumption of resources. The parklike grounds are as manicured as the rest of the yards in the community, not surprising given the number of professionals living in the community and the scores of gardeners who regularly descend on the

71

town. The children look much as other kids, and the surrounding community is filled with upper-middle-class housing developments. This school is in a wealthy suburban community, in fact, the most affluent in the state. Nelson Poole has been the principal at Sandburg for 6 years. He finished his master's and doctorate at Cornell. Dr. Poole, as everyone calls him, has the reputation of being a bright, conscientious, and hardworking principal. He puts in long hours, and few question his commitment to his school. And make no mistake about it, Nelson considered Sandburg his school.

Let's take a look at Sandburg Middle School. First, we examine the climate profiles as described by Dr. Poole. In other words, the following profile is the way Poole described the interactions in his school. He responded to the OHI-M and the OCDQ-RM and followed the directions in scoring the instruments. Poole also had his teachers respond to the same instruments at a faculty meeting. He took pains to get a frank response from the teachers by absenting himself from the meeting and insisting that teachers provide candid responses to the anonymous questionnaires. A comparison of the climate profiles as perceived by the teachers and Poole is found in Figures 6.1 and 6.2.

A quick glance at the profiles signals a problem. Poole describes a much better school than his teachers. Who is right? It doesn't matter. Poole has a problem because the teachers describe his behavior much more negatively than he thinks it is. For instance, he sees his leadership style as open, and his teachers perceive it as closed. His teachers describe him as much less supportive, less collegial, less influential, and more directive and restrictive than he does. Poole sees himself as a remarkably supportive and influential leader; his teachers do not. Interestingly, he also describes his teachers' behaviors much more positively than they do. The teachers describe the academic emphasis at Sandburg as average, but Poole sees it as high. The same is true of virtually every health indicator; Poole is a true pollyanna. Poole and his teachers seem to be describing different schools, but they are not. What's happening?

Identifying the problem and solving it call for different strategies. We have used our instruments to identify the problem. As it happens, that's the easy part. What to do is another matter. Poole has to find out why the teachers describe his behavior as more restrictive, directive, and nonsupportive than he thinks it is. Why does the faculty perceive virtually all interactions in the school as much less positive than Poole does? For example, why is it that the faculty doesn't see the collegial leadership that Poole is trying to model? Why does the faculty describe Dr. Poole's behavior as closed when he sees it as open? It seems clear that Nelson Poole is going to have to find a way to communicate with his faculty. This is not a problem he can solve by himself. It is an interaction issue. It may be a question of misperception. But who is misperceiving?

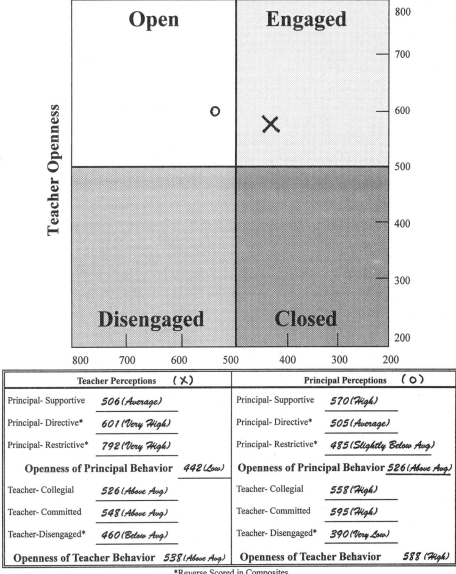

The following table appears within the figure:

Teacher Perceptions	(X)	Principal Perceptions	(O)
Principal- Supportive	*506 (Average)*	Principal- Supportive	*570 (High)*
Principal- Directive*	*601 (Very High)*	Principal- Directive*	*505 (Average)*
Principal- Restrictive*	*792 (Very High)*	Principal- Restrictive*	*485 (Slightly Below Avg)*
Openness of Principal Behavior	***442 (Low)***	**Openness of Principal Behavior**	***526 (Above Avg)***
Teacher- Collegial	*526 (Above Avg)*	Teacher- Collegial	*558 (High)*
Teacher- Committed	*548 (Above Avg)*	Teacher- Committed	*595 (High)*
Teacher-Disengaged*	*460 (Below Avg)*	Teacher- Disengaged*	*390 (Very Low)*
Openness of Teacher Behavior	***538 (Above Avg)***	**Openness of Teacher Behavior**	***588 (High)***

*Reverse Scored in Composites

Figure 6.1. Organizational Climate Description Questionnaire for Middle Schools (OCDQ-RM): Sandburg Middle School

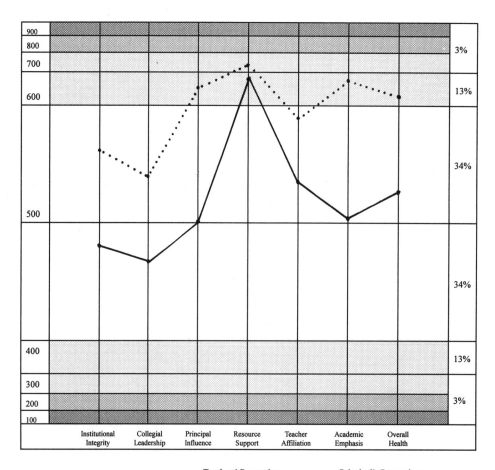

	Teachers' Perceptions	Principal's Perceptions
Institutional Integrity	481 (Slightly Below Avg)	560 (High)
Collegial Leadership	460 (Below Average)	535 (Above Average)
Principal Influence	501 (Average)	650 (Very High)
Resource Support	680 (Very High)	730 (Very High)
Teacher Affiliation	530 (High)	590 (High)
Academic Emphasis	505 (Average)	680 (Very High)
Overall Health	524 (Slightly Above Avg)	624 (Very High)

Figure 6.2. Organizational Health Inventory for Middle Schools (OHI-M): Sandburg Middle School

A Brief Digression: Some Assumptions About Change and Organizations

Before we proceed any further, we think it is useful to make clear some of the basic assumptions on which our analysis for change rests. The following assumptions are critical:

1. Change is a property of healthy and open organizations. The principal should see organizations in a constant state of flux. You cannot eliminate change from your school. Change happens, but it can be a random force or a resource harnessed for improvement.

2. Change has direction. Change can be progressive, regressive, or random. Schools should neither regress nor drift aimlessly. Progressive change is movement consistent with objectives and eventual solution of problems.

3. Organizational learning is possible. Schools can develop their own learning processes to solve their problems. Teachers and principals have high potential to learn how to solve problems together. However, they both need to see the organization as a whole and be aware of how change affects other parts of the system.

4. Schools should be learning organizations, places where "people continually expand their capacity to create the results that they truly desire, where new and expansive patterns of thinking are nurtured, where collective aspiration is set free, and where people are continually learning how to learn" (Senge, 1990, p. 3).

5. Healthy and open organizations are not only ends in themselves but also the means to learning organizations. Healthy and open schools are characterized by high levels of trust, commitment, and achievement, desirable in themselves. But the process of building school climate naturally transforms the school into a learning organization.

Organizational Development Model

What is a good strategy for ensuring healthy, open learning organizations? One useful method for changing school climate is a joint effort on the part of all those concerned, a so-called organizational development approach. Such a perspective addresses both personal and institutional needs and is a planned effort to make people and eventually organizations more productive (Hanson & Lubin, 1995). This sounds like an approach that might be useful for principals such as Poole who want to improve the health and openness of their school. To be successful, this strategy requires that individuals recognize difficulties and take responsibility for their solution. In the case at hand, the objective is to have teachers and the principal recognize that a challenge exists. Identifying the problem has been made manageable because the objective data clearly demonstrate discrepancies between the principal's and the teachers' perceptions of the social interactions in the workplace.

Before proceeding further, we outline the steps in an organizational development approach:

1. *Identify the problem*—discrepancies in the climate profiles.

2. *Establish a problem-solving team*—usually the teachers in the school. To change climate, teachers must be involved.

3. *The team takes on the problem*—the teachers and principal come to an understanding of the difficulty. Teachers examine the data with the principal and express a willingness to resolve the troubling issues. They must understand the situation and see the need for change.

4. *Diagnosis of the problem*—the team diagnoses the causes of the problem.

5. *Develop an action plan*—the team develops an action plan by examining alternatives, consequences, and then selecting a course of action.

6. *Implement the action plan*—put the plan into action.

7. *Evaluate*—assess the consequences of the plan by collecting new data and evaluating discrepancies.

Back to Sandburg School

Principal Nelson Poole was startled and dismayed by the school climate data. The teachers clearly see the school as much more negative than he does. This discrepancy in perceptions is a problem that needs to be addressed. Poole has identified the problem. Now he needs to establish a team to solve it. In other words, he needs to join forces with his teachers and involve them in organizational problem solving. Does this mean that he should involve all the teachers in the school? Probably, especially those who want to be part of the process and have something to say. Over the long run, the goal is to routinely have all teachers participate in decision making and organizational problem solving. Over the short run, the problem is putting together a team of leaders to begin the process.

An easy way to get teachers interested and involved is to use an inservice workshop for teachers. Most schools have a day or two throughout the year for such activities. First, teachers need to be made aware of the ideas of health and openness and how they are determined. Some time needs to be spent explicating the conceptual framework and measurement of school climate. In a faculty this small (33 teachers), the information could be given informally at the workshop with accompanying overheads and handouts to simplify the explanation. Our own experience in this regard is that teachers are very receptive to the climate ideas, especially because actual data about their school are available. They typically find the results of the OCDQ-RM and the OHI-M intriguing. And the process can be done in half a day. That is, by the end of the morning teachers should be able to examine overheads of profiles of school climates and describe in detail what they mean.

Next, teachers are ready to look at the profile of their own school as they have described it. The teachers' scores are standardized and presented. The teachers' score for general health is 524 (slightly above average); teacher openness is 538 (above average), but principal openness is 442 (low). From the teachers' vantage point, this is an engaged school: Behavior among the teachers is open and authentic, but interactions between the teachers and the principal are closed. Although the teachers described themselves as relatively open in their dealings with each other, they saw the principal as closed in dealing with them. Why was this? Before answering the question, Poole suggested that they examine his profile of the school's climate (see Figure 6.1). Now, the discrepancies became even more obvious because the principal saw his behavior as being open, whereas the faculty described it as closed (526 versus 442). Moreover, Poole saw the school as a very healthy place to work and learn, and the teachers described the school's health as slightly above average (624 versus 524). What's happening here? The principal needed to know, and so did the teachers.

This was a time for some straight talk. The principal must ascertain why the teachers saw his behavior as less supportive, more directive, and more restrictive than he did. Poole admitted to the faculty that he was puzzled by the results because he thought his relationship with the faculty was much more positive. Although he was perplexed, he was willing to examine his own values and choices in this public forum. This is not to say he was comfortable in doing so. He wasn't, but he felt constrained to discuss the findings because it was his idea to begin with. At this stage, he had some reservations about the whole project, but he felt he had no choice but to move forward. He tried to convince himself that he needed to have an experimental attitude toward his own behavior and toward the interactions with his teacher colleagues. He had to take some risks to improve the climate of the school, or, at the very least, get his teachers and himself on "the same page." Above all, he wanted a climate of openness and trust in which learning would be continuous. Poole was shaken but determined.

Actually, the problem-solving process was not as dramatic as one might think. There were, after all, only 33 teachers on the faculty, and they had not said that the school was bad, only that Poole was too directive and restrictive in his leadership. This was not terrible, but it was bad enough. Poole and the teachers must seek explanations and avoid blaming or scapegoating. Was the problem real? Of course, and the teachers recognized it.

Poole and his teachers had an open conversation about the causes of the discrepancies. Let's listen in:

Poole: I was surprised that the faculty thought vocal parents had easy entrée to the school. I don't think you realize the number of parents whom I divert at the front office. We don't have real dissatisfaction in the community, but there are people who feel the faculty should have to hear what they want to say about the education of their kids.

Faculty member: Well, it's true we don't know how much you do, but we do know how many parents come to see us and complain about things we can't do anything about. It's not a big problem, but it's annoying.

Poole: What do you mean? Give me an example.

Faculty member: Look, the kids get high marks on the Iowa tests, and yet parents stream in to complain that the scores should be higher. Not everyone can be in the 99th percentile, even here.

Poole: I can't isolate you from the community.

Faculty member: We know that! But it's interference nonetheless, and we think you can do better. That's why our scores on institutional integrity differ from yours.

Poole: What do you think I can do? Parents have a right to come into the school.

Faculty member: Of course they have a right to come in. But we would like you to head them off and explain about test scores and percentiles.

(Long period of silence)

Poole: Well, well, . . . well, I'll try. We need to talk about this some more. I do understand why we responded to the items on institutional integrity differently. That's useful. But what really surprised me, and I don't understand, was our wholly different views of my leadership. I think of myself as being a lot more supportive and open than you give me credit for.

(Long period of silence)

Faculty member: Well, we do think of you as supportive, but you lay all sorts of directives and paperwork on us. It's just too much.

Poole: Give me an example.

Faculty member: To be blunt, you don't give us enough freedom to make the decisions that we need to make. You're an old English teacher, and I am a veteran mathematics teacher. Why do you think you know more about solving quadratic equations than I do?

Poole: I never said I did.

Faculty member: Well, maybe not, but you leave that kind of impression every time you observe my class. Here's what I mean: I am struggling in class with one of the slower students trying to get him up to speed on work we covered 2 weeks ago. And you suggest that I should give students more chances to discover relationships. You claim that I need to be more indirect in my instruction. You just don't understand what's happening in the class.

Poole: I do have other responsibilities, but I am concerned about this problem.

Another faculty member: I agree with Bill. You need to treat us more as professionals and less as subordinates. You're a smart guy and you work hard. But you don't see us as equals. You treat us as hired help.

Poole: I don't want to hurt your feelings, but when things go wrong, I'm the one accountable. I take the heat, so I want things to run as well as possible.

Faculty member: You asked for some examples, and you just got two. What are you going to do?

Poole: Well, I'll have to think about this. I appreciate your candor, but it's hard for me not to be defensive. We may have to change some things.

This little exchange should give you a flavor of the kind of conversation that may likely occur. A close analysis of the conversation shows that the principal himself sees a difference in his status, and he indirectly communicates it ("I'm the one accountable"). Teachers are seeking more autonomy, and some teachers feel the principal doesn't respect their expertise. In other parts of the dialogue, it also became obvious that many teachers felt that occasionally Poole's observations of their performance were critical but neither insightful nor constructive. Moreover, many believed that Poole rarely respected their professional judgments. These were some of the reasons for the discrepancies between Poole's perception of his leadership style and the faculty's perceptions.

What are the causes of these discrepancies? It is at this point that the principal and teachers developed a series of rival explanations for the differences in perceptions. The teachers had to be willing to take some risks in articulating their position without fear of reprisal. The teachers were divided into three groups, and each developed an explanation of what was happening. The principal was not part of any group. But rather, Poole also developed a tentative explanation of the data. After an hour or so, the group as a whole reassembled, and the four explanations were presented and compared. Now, the principal's chore was to work with the faculty toward some consensus on causes. If no consensus could be reached, then each reasonable explanation should be tested in the weeks and months ahead.

There were four groups, the principal and his assistant and three faculty groups, developing explanations of the discrepancies between the principal and the faculty. After comparing the explanations, the faculty agreed on the following diagnosis:

Parents were going directly to the teachers with their criticisms and demands. There was agreement that Poole needed to serve as a buffer between parents and the teachers. Growing out of conversations of the kind that we have just heard, the teachers suggested that Poole would be seen as more collegial and supportive if he would delegate more responsibility and autonomy to them, treat them as full-fledged professionals, and consult more often. A goodly number of teachers also offered that busywork, such as written, formal lesson plans that go unreviewed, be eliminated. They suggested a committee on paperwork whose charge was to reduce paperwork wherever feasible. For his part, Poole still did not share the explanation of his faculty, but he respected the faculty's judgments and agreed that something needed to be done and he would do it.

Both Poole and the teachers thought that the resource support for teachers was exceptional. Poole saw it as stronger than the teachers but not critically so. Indeed, in the final analysis, everyone felt good about the resource support of the school. The teachers believed that teacher affiliation was lower than Poole observed because although the teachers were friendly and trusting of each other, at the end of the day they went their separate ways. The teachers agreed that academic emphasis at Sandburg was about average. Poole, however, was unaware that for at least half the teachers, student homework and apathy were problems. Poole was probably mislead by the high achievement scores of many students. The students were bright, but not especially committed to academics. Social activities were more important to many students than academic ones.

When it came to the openness of teachers and their relationships, Poole and the teachers more or less agreed that the faculty was open. But there was room for improvement. Although the teachers were committed and engaged in their behavior, they were only above average in collegiality; there was potential for growth here.

There were sharp discrepancies between Poole's and the faculty's perceptions of directive and restrictive behavior of the principal. By and large, the teachers believed that his observations of their classroom teaching were perfunctory and harsh. He didn't visit the classrooms often, but when he did, he always had many directives for improvement. The teachers resented the style if not the substance of his comments. The teachers resented the formal sign in and sign out required of all teachers. This was a relatively small school, and everyone knew when others came and went. The teachers resented the extreme formalization in the school—there were parking forms, library materials forms, AV equipment forms, grade distribution forms, repetitive absentee forms, lateness forms, lunch forms, and even a form for the number of minutes spent helping kids after school (which was, after all, a volunteer activity). Teachers found the forms to be restrictive and for the most part unnecessary. Poole saw the forms as a quick way to keep track of things.

How do we develop constructive plans for reducing discrepancies and improving climate? This is the time for the teachers and the principal to work together to forge a realistic plan. There is no one best way to do this, but in the current case the principal and teachers decided to each work on the plan independently and then come back together (much in the same manner as they had framed the causes of the problem) to propose a school improvement plan.

The faculty inservice meeting to discuss and formulate an improvement plan was interesting, to say the least. In response to the analysis of problem causes, the principal thought that he might do the following:

1. Poole at first suggested that the teachers notify his office about instances of parental interference, however the faculty might judge it. Poole would monitor the reports and said if the problem got out of hand, he would step in to buffer the teachers from the parents.

2. Poole was genuinely concerned about the appearance of a heavy-handed insensitive administration. He proposed to study the amount of paperwork and forms required and reduce them dramatically. He pledged to consult and listen to his teachers before acting. He thought highly of his teachers and conceded that they should have more independence in making professional judgments. In fact, he proposed that a leadership cabinet be formed composed of all the team leaders to share in decision making in the school. Finally, he proposed that the team leaders and the teachers should develop a program of peer supervision. In essence, Poole proposed a delegation of authority and responsibility to his teachers. Although he thought lesson plans were necessary to ensure a coherent curriculum, he was willing to delegate this responsibility to teachers and team leaders.

3. The discrepancy between Poole's perception of teacher collegiality and the teachers' judgment probably erred on the side of optimism and seemed of no great consequence. Poole may have overgeneralized about the teachers, but he was determined to involve his teachers in collaborative efforts in which they enjoyed working with each other professionally. To that end, he proposed that the next inservice day be devoted to developing strategies for joint curriculum development across interdisciplinary teams.

4. Poole promised that he would make himself more readily available to the faculty. He also pledged that in the future, his criticism would be constructive and helpful. He concluded by reaffirming confidence and admiration for his faculty and pointed out the one area in

which there was virtual agreement was the commitment of the teachers to the students.

5. Finally, Poole was concerned about the academic seriousness of the school. This was a good school in a community that supported education. He was shocked to find his teachers did not share his perception of the academic climate of Sandburg Middle School. He vowed to address the issue on a number of fronts. First, a series of meetings with his faculty were necessary to discover the origin of the faculty's assessment of the mediocre academic press at Sandburg.

The faculty for its part came in with the following set of recommendations:

1. The teachers proposed that Poole become actively involved as a liaison between teachers and parents. In particular, they recommended that the team leaders together with Poole and the executive committee of the PTA meet regularly to address and mollify parental concerns.

2. The teachers proposed a system of peer-group coaching to improve the teaching-learning process. They asked that they be given more input into future inservice meetings.

3. Because Sandburg was such a small school, the faculty proposed that the principal consult with them informally about important school issues. They didn't want more meetings, just more influence and information.

4. The teachers recommended that a committee of teachers be appointed to streamline the bureaucratic procedures of the school— no more forms.

5. The teachers recommended that a schoolwide policy be established on homework and tutorials. The honor society would be approached and asked to do volunteer tutoring a few afternoons a week.

After the suggestions and recommendations were enumerated and discussed, Poole and the faculty were concerned about the number of different issues that surfaced and the time needed to confront them. Poole for his part admitted that he was unrealistically optimistic and the whole exercise provided him with a reality check. The teachers, on the other hand, were a little afraid that if they tried to do too much, nothing would be accomplished. They needed a reasonable plan that was realistic and attainable. There was, however, an inherent dilemma in their suggestions: They wanted greater involvement and more interaction but fewer meetings and less administrative work. They agreed to be idealistic and yet pragmatic. The following aspects were key elements of their eventual plan.

1. Four teachers volunteered to work with the principal to find ways to reduce paperwork, unnecessary meetings, and administrative routine.

2. Poole and the teachers agreed that team leaders, the executive committee of the PTA, and Poole would meet regularly to address community concerns.

3. Formal lesson plans were eliminated as a requirement, but the teachers agreed to have an outline of the class activities for the week. They also agreed that when one was absent, they would help each other by aiding the substitute and by keeping in touch with the absent teacher. Team leaders were given the responsibility of coordinating this process.

4. Poole agreed with the teachers that a system of peer coaching should be initiated. Teachers agreed to combine classes on occasion so that they could serve as teaching models and coaches for each other.

5. The faculty and Poole agreed that a leadership cabinet composed of team leaders and elected teachers should be formed to share in the governance of the school. Poole agreed to consult with the faculty cabinet concerning all matters in which teachers had a personal stake and professional knowledge. Poole suggested and teachers agreed that the faculty would have complete independence in planning the programs for the 3 inservice days of professional development next year.

Clearly, this plan is not a set of step-by-step procedures to be accomplished in a rigid way. To the contrary, the plan is a set of accepted guidelines and commitments.

How will this plan be implemented? Lesson plans will be eliminated as a formal requirement immediately (Item 3). The paperwork committee (Item 1), as the teachers called it, agreed to meet in the next several weeks and would have recommendations back to the faculty and principal in 2 months. Another committee of teachers would be formed to plan the specifics for the peer-coaching experiment (Item 4). The principal decided to set aside a portion of each regular faculty meeting for faculty governance (Item 5). The teachers and principal realize that their plan requires increased effort. It is ironic that a major goal of the plan is to reduce unnecessary meetings, yet the cost of involvement, professional control, and autonomy is more meetings. The faculty is committed to the plan even though they know it will be more work, but meaningful work.

How successful would this plan be? That is an empirical question. In 6 months, two activities would occur to assess its effectiveness. First, the OCDQ-RM and OHI-M would be administered and scored, and then the principal and faculty would revisit the climate and changes at Sandburg.

Just to keep things in perspective, let us review what has happened in the inservice at Sandburg. The morning of the first day was spent explaining, discussing, and interpreting the climate frameworks, their measures, and the school profiles. In the afternoon, the teachers were confronted with the openness and health profiles of Sandburg. After some discussion of those profiles and agreement on what they meant, the principal introduced his perception of the school profile, which diverged dramatically from that of the faculty. The discrepancies led to a frank and open discussion between the principal and teachers culminating in the formation of three teacher groups to develop tentative explanations about the causes of the discrepancies in perceptions. After working in small groups for an hour or so, the teachers reconvened and shared their explanations, coming to a rough consensus about the causes of the discrepancy. The next day was spent formulating a plan to reduce the discrepancies and improve the health and openness of the school. These two inservice days should be thought of as a beginning of a continuous program of improvement and problem solving. Even if these educators are successful in developing the school climate they all desire, periodic monitoring of climate is a wise course. We hope that through this process two things occur: first, that the climate of the school is improved, and second, that group problem solving and organizational learning become natural elements of school life.

Taft Senior High School: Discrepancy Between Actual and Desired Profile

Taft Senior High School is a suburban school enrolling approximately 2,500 students. Taft High School is in an old town on the outskirts of a large northeastern city. Its population, about 50,000, is a mix of different ethnic groups. Some had moved years earlier from the larger city to the suburbs and retain much of their ethnic affiliation. Others, from skilled blue-collar- and middle-class professional occupations, are recent residents.

Edward "Ted" McMann had been principal at Taft for 6 years. McMann had been a teacher in the school system for 20 years before being appointed principal over the strong challenge of two able and experienced candidates from outside the system. He was a well-liked social studies teacher and coach before he was appointed assistant principal 10 years earlier. Ted knows the faculty well; in fact, his tenure in the district has made him an "old-timer." Since becoming principal, he surprised a good number of his colleagues with his progressive ideas and initiatives. He hired an assistant principal who instituted curriculum innovation, returned to graduate school for advanced study in administration, fostered a multicultural curriculum in social studies, and took preliminary steps to develop shared decision making with the faculty. Indeed, his progressive ideas sometimes raised eyebrows among members of the board of education. His relationship with the new superintendent was proper but not warm. Superintendent Sylvia McClelland was still getting to know the district and inclined to be a little careful. McMann was feeling a little tentative himself.

His contacts at the university and his reading of the popular literature had introduced him to the concepts of culture and climate. He thought he had a good school with a good climate, but he sensed something was amiss at Taft so he decided to test his suspicion. To that end, he administered the OCDQ-RS to half of his faculty and the OHI to the other half at a recent faculty meeting. He took pains to ensure that the teacher respondents were anonymous; no name or number appeared on the questionnaires. He had the guidance counselor administer and collect the information in his absence. The teachers were informed that the survey was to take a "snapshot" of the school climate and guaranteed that they would receive the results. The faculty did, indeed, enjoy responding to the instruments in the 10 minutes that it took. Actually, various items sparked discussion among some teachers after the meeting.

When Ted McMann looked at the scores (see Figure 6.3), his suspicions were confirmed. Why was academic emphasis so low? In fact, not only did the low score for academic emphasis bother him, but he was also annoyed by the overall mediocrity of the school. This was not a bad school, but then again, neither was it as excellent as McMann felt it should be. The openness and health indexes tell the story—this was an average school, about as average as you can get. As you may recall, a standardized score of 500 is at the absolute midpoint of the distribution of typical high schools.

Not only did the low academic emphasis puzzle him, but he found the low principal influence score particularly galling because he prided himself on his successful relations with the central office and the board. The teachers were just wrong! But their misperception was his problem. Moreover, neither the overall health nor openness of the climate was as high as McMann thought it should be. Given the fact of his supportive leadership, why weren't teachers more engaged in the teaching task? Why wasn't morale higher? What was frustrating them?

McMann was dismayed. What should he do? He felt better about the school before he had the data. Maybe ignorance was bliss. But he had started the ball rolling and there was no turning back. At the next faculty meeting, McMann took the bull by the horns and presented the data to the faculty. He needed about a half an hour to first develop the conceptual basis of these climate instruments. Then he interpreted the findings to the faculty using a series of overheads. He was a little surprised that the teachers simply nodded in agreement. At this point, McMann felt compelled to comment on his dissatisfaction with the profile. Slowly, a few teachers began

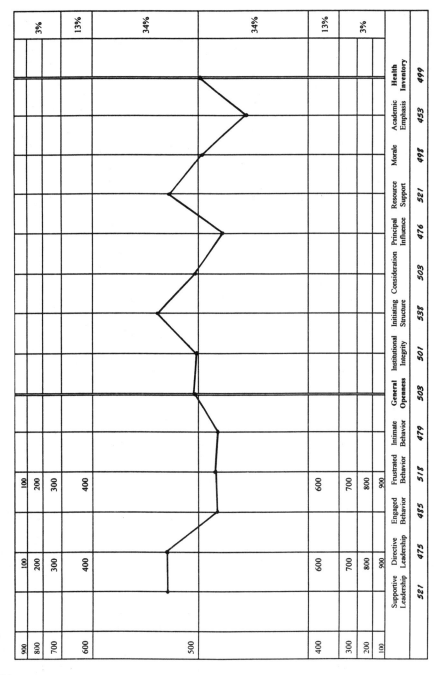

Figure 6.3. Openness (OCDQ-RS) and Health (OHI-S) Profile: Taft High School

also to voice discontent at the findings. "What should we do?" he asked. He knew the question was a mistake as soon as the question left his lips. What ensued was a rambling series of diatribes, half accusations and half self-flagellation. During the meeting, he realized that this was not the right forum. One hundred and fifty teachers can't adequately discuss the findings in any useful fashion. Besides, things were getting out of hand. He cut off discussion and moved ahead on his full agenda.

The next morning, McMann reflected on the meeting. Most people agreed that the profile was fairly accurate, but the reasons for it were confused. He decided to push the issue further at the next meeting of the administrative cabinet (composed of department chairs and assistant principals). At the meeting, he would propose that a representative and interested group of teachers be asked to work with him in analyzing the causes for the mediocre scores and in drafting a plan to improve the climate of the school. His administrative cabinet was receptive to this idea and agreed to ask for volunteers from each department and to give a push to a few people they felt should be on such a committee; no one was to be excluded.

Fifteen people eventually were identified and agreed to serve on the committee. All departments were represented and no department had more than three members on the committee. As McMann looked over the list of faculty, he was pleased. They were all concerned teachers whom he considered to be some of his best. Most were leaders in their respective departments, although a few were new faculty. The first meeting was held after school about a month later. During that initial meeting, it became obvious that much more time was necessary to evaluate the results and develop a plan of action. Later, McMann spoke with the superintendent and made a case for organizational development in his school. Without going into the details, he was able to get the superintendent to agree to underwrite a modest stipend for faculty participation on the organizational development (OD) committee, as it was now called. McMann felt it would be more productive for the OD committee to meet on a few Saturdays at Taft. He spoke informally with most of the committee members and they agreed to come in for at least a few meetings.

The first of these meetings lasted about 3 hours. The first hour was spent reviewing the conceptual underpinnings of the climate framework. Then, a general discussion about the specific climate at Taft ended with the committee breaking into three groups to diagnose the causes of the problems. What were the problems? They had decided that academic emphasis was much too low, the principal needed to exert more leadership with the superintendent and board, and the faculty should be less frustrated and more engaged. They saw no difficulty with the institutional integrity of the school, and except for his influence with superiors, they lauded McMann for his reality-oriented leadership. Although intimacy was relatively low, the faculty was unconcerned and reasoned that the outcome was a function of the large size of the school. In sum, the committee decided to focus on finding the causes for limited success in academic emphasis, principal in-fluence, teacher engagement, teacher frustration, and overall morale. In other words, the task the committee set for itself was to find the causes of the problems and eliminate them.

Before proceeding any further, let's review where we are in our OD approach and how we got there. The administration's analysis of the climate instruments revealed some major discrepancies between what existed at Taft and what McMann and the faculty desired. After an aborted attempt to deal with the problem at a faculty meeting, McMann initiated proce-dures to form a school improvement team, which in this school turned out to be called the OD committee. Remember, the school improvement team was a group of teacher volunteers representing all departments in the school. They volunteered because they believed the school had problems but also the potential to overcome them. In other words, the team took on the problem as its own.

The next phase of the school improvement process is to diagnose the causes of the problem. To this end, the OD committee met for four consecu-tive Saturday mornings. They divided themselves into four teams, each team with a specific charge to analyze a problem area and recommend a solution: Bill DesLauriers, from the science department, led a group to ana-lyze the academic emphasis problem and propose possible actions. Megan O'Donnell, from the English department, was charged with the problem of low teacher engagement. Wayne Washington, from foreign languages, headed up the group concerned with the difficulty of the limited influence of the principal (they invited Principal McMann to be part of their group). Finally, Brett Bergamo, from social studies, worked with his committee to attack the issue of teacher frustration.

We briefly summarize the work and findings of the team. DesLauriers's team found that low academic emphasis had many roots. First, there was little recognition of students who excelled. Second, there was little consis-tent policy among departments concerning student requirements. One de-partment had rigid homework requirements, another frowned on too much homework, and the others were indifferent. Some departments maintained a tight control over students; others were more lax, some would say permissive. The result was the students sometimes viewed get-ting along with the faculty as more important than asking questions in class. Some teachers seemed to give high grades for anything; others sel-dom gave grades above B+. Many students negotiated an easy path through the programs. Through interviews and anecdotes, it also became clear to the team that there were a few teachers who simply didn't put in the kind of time and effort necessary for effective teaching. A surprise for the team emerged when it became apparent that faculty had modest expec-tations for most students; they simply didn't think many students could do rigorous work.

The recommendations the committee presented were as follows:

1. An annual assembly would be held to recognize honor students; student academic successes would be publicized monthly in the school paper.

2. Each interdisciplinary team would be asked to formalize and share its policies on homework. The committee agreed that there should be high but achievable expectations for all students and such standards should be public.

3. The team leaders agreed to work with their faculty to develop a handbook on student conduct to encourage honesty and individual responsibility.

4. Although the committee agreed that some teachers were not working very hard, they decided against any formal statement or action but instead encouraged each other to work informally with the slackers.

O'Donnell's team was perplexed that some teachers didn't spend enough time helping students and were indifferent to student needs. Many of these teachers seemed to begrudge their colleagues' enthusiasm and yet apparently felt put upon because they believed that many of the engaged teachers looked down their noses at them. Too many teachers did not take pride in the school because of the mediocre performance of students.

After much discussion and some lively arguments, O'Donnell's committee could only agree on two recommendations.

1. They recommended that teachers be required to work with students after school for half an hour every day. They went so far as to suggest that the union leadership be involved in efforts to encourage faculty help with homework and academic tutoring.

2. To get faculty and students to be proud of their school, both must perform at a higher level. Success breeds pride. As a first step, the committee recommended that a student learning center be established to help students achieve at a higher level. The center would be funded by the board of education and a few large local businesses. Second, an outreach committee should be established to involve parents in the support of both the football program and the marching band.

Wayne Washington's group was surprised that Principal McMann thought he was so influential with the central office. Most teachers didn't agree. They could think of little evidence that suggested otherwise. In fact, McMann had been criticized publicly by the several board members.

Moreover, Washington's team was unaware of McMann's involvement in the civic organizations of the community. In point of fact, he was the chairman of the YMCA executive council, an active Rotarian, and a member of an interdenominational alliance for civic improvement, to mention only a few connections. Indeed, the committee was not only surprised by his ties to the life of the town, but encouraged Principal McMann to share his involvement with the faculty at large.

Washington's team made two recommendations:

1. The principal and superintendent should conduct a forum periodically with the teachers at Taft to explain policy and listen to teacher ideas and suggestions.

2. The principal should make visible his activity in local civic organizations by talking briefly to the teachers about those activities and developing a quarterly newsletter that highlighted school-community relations.

Brett Bergamo's team found that much of the frustration teachers experienced arose from a plethora of requirements for formal notes to the office about student absences, deportment, inventories, and club activities. These notes—too small to call reports—often took up an exorbitant amount of time in the opinion of many faculty members. Teachers objected to having to sign in at the office every morning, they objected to monthly faculty meetings because they were not all necessary, they objected to cafeteria duty and hall patrol, and they objected to the elaborate record keeping for absenteeism and tardiness.

Bergamo's team joked that in response to too many administrative duties, the team formed a new committee. They made the following recommendations:

1. A committee should be appointed to streamline record keeping for students.

2. Teacher sign-in should be abolished and teachers should be required to call in only if they were going to be late or absent.

3. Aides should be hired to monitor the hall and cafeteria.

These team reports and recommendations were made on the third Saturday meeting, and the entire group decided to meet one more time to formulate a plan of action. Eleven recommendations were proposed by the teams. Everyone agreed that the agenda was too ambitious over the short run and that a narrower focus should be developed. Several recommendations were eliminated or postponed after a systematic analysis of their likely success. The recommendation that teachers be required to work with students after school was eliminated as being too disruptive and alienating to teachers. Over the short term, the group agreed that convincing the board to hire aides to monitor the hall and cafeteria was wishful thinking.

Several recommendations were immediately feasible. First, the principal agreed to abolish teacher sign in. Second, a committee to streamline record keeping would be appointed within a month. Third, the members of the OD committee would informally initiate efforts to help their colleagues and set an example of commitment to the school and students. Fourth, the principal and superintendent would have voluntary bimonthly forums for interested teachers. Fifth, the principal agreed to publish a quarterly newsletter to parents and teachers about school-community activities. Sixth, several new committees would also be appointed—a student handbook committee, an assembly committee to honor academic achievement, a homework committee, and an outreach committee. Finally, the principal agreed to work with the superintendent and civic leaders to develop support for a student learning center that would provide small group and private tutoring as well as computer-aided instruction.

Another spontaneous suggestion emerged that seemed worth exploring. One teacher jokingly commented that to promote goodwill in the community, the teachers should propose a "Contract With the Citizens." That comment led to the possibility that perhaps the teachers in the high school should draft and sign a public pledge to citizens in which they reaffirm their commitment to teaching, learning, good citizenship, honesty, and civility. Some agreed it was an interesting idea, but all agreed it was an issue for another time.

A tentative plan of action was clear. In fact, the implementation of the plan seemed straightforward. What remained to be determined was its success, which would be evaluated next year at the same time using the OCDQ-RS and OHI-S.

Schools like Sandburg and Taft are quite good to begin with; they have enlightened principals. The road to school improvement, even in good schools, is usually slow and arduous, but with reflective administrators and faculty involvement and commitment, it is possible. Sometimes the problems are too large and complex for schools to address on their own. In these instances, we suggest that the administration consider bringing in an OD consultant to help the schools in the process of change.

A Concluding Comment

With this book, you have in your hands the tools that you will need to assess the openness and health of your school. The data you gather from these measures can have a significant effect if commitment to school improvement is combined with a leader who is prepared to develop an inclusive process of change. With improved climate, you can look forward to other related outcomes such as increased faculty commitment, faculty trust, and eventually increased student achievement. It won't be easy. Constructive change rarely is; it has its costs. We believe, however, the results of such analyses and improvement plans will produce a more productive and positive school environment for students, teachers, administrators, and parents.

Appendix A
Instrument, Dimensions, and Profile Chart for OCDQ-RM

OCDQ-RM

Directions: The following are statements about your school. Please indicate the extent to which each statement characterizes your school by circling the appropriate response.

RO = rarely occurs; SO = sometimes occurs; O = often occurs; VFO = very frequently occurs

1.	The principal compliments teachers.	RO SO O VFO
2.	Teachers have parties for each other.	RO SO O VFO
3.	Teachers are burdened with busy work.	RO SO O VFO
4.	Routine duties interfere with the job of teaching.	RO SO O VFO
5.	Teachers "go the extra mile" with their students.	RO SO O VFO
6.	Teachers are committed to helping their students.	RO SO O VFO
7.	Teachers help students on their own time.	RO SO O VFO
8.	Teachers interrupt other teachers who are talking in staff meetings.	RO SO O VFO
9.	The principal rules with an iron fist.	RO SO O VFO
10.	The principal encourages teacher autonomy.	RO SO O VFO
11.	The principal goes out of his or her way to help teachers.	RO SO O VFO
12.	The principal is available after school to help teachers when assistance is needed.	RO SO O VFO
13.	Teachers invite other faculty members to visit them at home.	RO SO O VFO
14.	Teachers socialize with each other on a regular basis.	RO SO O VFO
15.	The principal uses constructive criticism.	RO SO O VFO
16.	Teachers who have personal problems receive support from other staff members.	RO SO O VFO
17.	Teachers stay after school to tutor students who need help.	RO SO O VFO
18.	Teachers accept additional duties if students will benefit.	RO SO O VFO
19.	The principal looks out for the personal welfare of teachers.	RO SO O VFO
20.	The principal supervises teachers closely.	RO SO O VFO
21.	Teachers leave school immediately after school is over.	RO SO O VFO
22.	Most of the teachers here accept the faults of their colleagues.	RO SO O VFO
23.	Teachers exert group pressure on nonconforming faculty members.	RO SO O VFO
24.	The principal listens to and accepts teachers' suggestions.	RO SO O VFO
25.	Teachers have fun socializing together during school time.	RO SO O VFO
26.	Teachers ramble when they talk at faculty meetings.	RO SO O VFO
27.	Teachers are rude to other staff members.	RO SO O VFO
28.	Teachers make wisecracks to each other during meetings.	RO SO O VFO
29.	Teachers mock teachers who are different.	RO SO O VFO
30.	Teachers don't listen to other teachers.	RO SO O VFO

Hoy and Tarter. *The Road to Open and Healthy Schools: A Handbook for Change, Middle and Secondary School Edition.* Copyright © 1997, Corwin Press, Inc.

OCDQ-RM (Continued)

31. Teachers like to hear gossip about other staff members.		RO SO O VFO
32. The principal treats teachers as equals.		RO SO O VFO
33. The principal corrects teachers' mistakes.		RO SO O VFO
34. Teachers provide strong social support for colleagues.		RO SO O VFO
35. Teachers respect the professional competence of their colleagues.		RO SO O VFO
36. The principal goes out of his or her way to show appreciation to teachers.		RO SO O VFO
37. The principal keeps a close check on sign-in times.		RO SO O VFO
38. The principal monitors everything teachers do.		RO SO O VFO
39. Administrative paperwork is burdensome at this school.		RO SO O VFO
40. Teachers help and support each other.		RO SO O VFO
41. The principal closely checks teacher activities.		RO SO O VFO
42. Assigned nonteaching duties are excessive.		RO SO O VFO
43. The interactions between team/unit members are cooperative.		RO SO O VFO
44. The principal accepts and implements ideas suggested by faculty members.		RO SO O VFO
45. Members of teams/units consider other members to be their friends.		RO SO O VFO
46. Extra help is available to students who need help.		RO SO O VFO
47. Teachers volunteer to sponsor after-school activities.		RO SO O VFO
48. Teachers spend time after school with students who have individual problems.		RO SO O VFO
49. The principal sets an example by working hard himself or herself.		RO SO O VFO
50. Teachers are polite to each other.		RO SO O VFO

SOURCE: James Hoffman, *The Organizational Climate of Middle Schools and Dimensions of Authenticity and Trust*. (Unpublished doctoral dissertation, Rutgers University, New Brunswick, New Jersey, 1993.) Used with permission.

Dimensions of Organizational Climate (OCDQ-RM)

Principal's Behavior

Supportive behavior is directed toward both the social needs and task achievement of faculty. The principal is helpful, genuinely concerned with teachers, and attempts to motivate by using constructive criticism and by setting an example through hard work.

Directive behavior is rigid, domineering behavior. The principal maintains close and constant monitoring over virtually all aspects of teacher behavior in the school.

Restrictive behavior is behavior that hinders, rather than facilitates, teacher work. The principal burdens teachers with paperwork, committee requirements, and other demands that interfere with their teaching responsibilities.

Teachers' Behavior

Collegial behavior supports open and professional interactions among teachers. Teachers like, respect, and help one another both professionally and personally.

Committed behavior is directed toward helping students to develop both socially and intellectually. Teachers work extra hard to ensure student success in school.

Disengaged behavior signifies a lack of meaning and focus to professional activities. Teachers simply are putting in their time; in fact, they are critical and unaccepting of their colleagues.

OCDQ-RM
Organizational Climate Description Questionnaire for Middle Schools

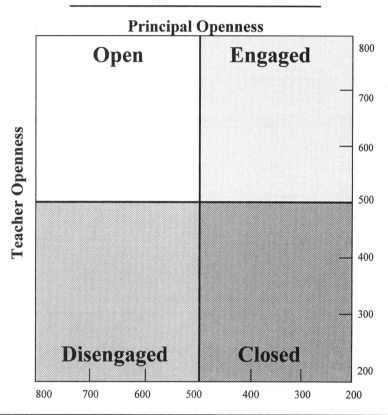

Principal Openness

Open	**Engaged**
Disengaged	**Closed**

Teacher Openness

800
700
600
500
400
300
200

800 700 600 500 400 300 200

Teacher Perceptions			Principal Perceptions		
Principal- Supportive			Principal- Supportive		
Principal- Directive*			Principal- Directive*		
Principal- Restrictive*			Principal- Restrictive*		
Openness of Principal Behavior			**Openness of Principal Behavior**		
Teacher- Collegial			Teacher- Collegial		
Teacher- Committed			Teacher- Committed		
Teacher- Disengaged*			Teacher- Disengaged*		
Openness of Teacher Behavior			**Openness of Teacher Behavior**		
Total Openness			**Total Openness**		

*Reverse Scored in Composites

Hoy and Tarter. *The Road to Open and Healthy Schools: A Handbook for Change,
Middle and Secondary School Edition.* Copyright © 1997, Corwin Press, Inc.

Appendix B
Instrument, Dimensions, and Profile Chart for OHI-M

OHI-M

Directions: The following are statements about your school. Please indicate the extent to which each statement characterizes your school by circling the appropriate response.

RO = rarely occurs; SO = sometimes occurs; O = often occurs; VFO = very frequently occurs

1. The principal explores all sides of topics and admits
    that other options exist.   RO SO O VFO
2. Students make provisions to acquire extra help from
    teachers.   RO SO O VFO
3. The principal gets what he or she asks for from superiors.   RO SO O VFO
4. The principal discusses classroom issues with teachers.   RO SO O VFO
5. The principal accepts questions without appearing to
    snub or quash the teacher.   RO SO O VFO
6. Extra materials are available if requested.   RO SO O VFO
7. Students neglect to complete homework.   RO SO O VFO
8. The school is vulnerable to outside pressures.   RO SO O VFO
9. The principal is able to influence the actions of his or
    her superiors.   RO SO O VFO
10. The principal treats all faculty members as his or her equal. RO SO O VFO
11. Teachers are provided with adequate materials for their
    classrooms.   RO SO O VFO
12. Teachers in this school like each other.   RO SO O VFO
13. Community demands are accepted even when they
    are not consistent with the educational program.   RO SO O VFO
14. The principal lets faculty know what is expected of them.   RO SO O VFO
15. Teachers receive necessary classroom supplies.   RO SO O VFO
16. Students respect others who get good grades.   RO SO O VFO
17. Good grades are important to the students of this school.   RO SO O VFO
18. Teachers feel pressure from the community.   RO SO O VFO
19. The principal's recommendations are given serious
    consideration by his or her superiors.   RO SO O VFO
20. Supplementary materials are available for classroom use.   RO SO O VFO
21. Teachers exhibit friendliness to each other.   RO SO O VFO
22. Students seek extra work so they can get good grades.   RO SO O VFO
23. Select citizen groups are influential with the board.   RO SO O VFO
24. The principal looks out for the personal welfare of
    faculty members.   RO SO O VFO
25. The school is open to the whims of the public.   RO SO O VFO
26. A few vocal parents can change school policy.   RO SO O VFO
27. Students try hard to improve on previous work.   RO SO O VFO
28. Teachers accomplish their jobs with enthusiasm.   RO SO O VFO
29. The learning environment is orderly and serious.   RO SO O VFO
30. The principal is friendly and approachable.   RO SO O VFO

OHI-M (Continued)

31. Teachers show commitment to their students.   RO SO O VFO
32. Teachers are indifferent to each other.   RO SO O VFO
33. Teachers are protected from unreasonable community
    and parental demands.   RO SO O VFO
34. The principal is able to work well with the superintendent.   RO SO O VFO
35. The principal is willing to make changes.   RO SO O VFO
36. Teachers have access to needed instructional materials.   RO SO O VFO
37. Teachers in this school are cool and aloof to each other.   RO SO O VFO
38. Teachers in this school believe that their students have
    the ability to achieve academically.   RO SO O VFO
39. The principal is understanding when personal concerns
    cause teachers to arrive late or leave early.   RO SO O VFO
40. Our school gets its fair share of resources from the district.   RO SO O VFO
41. The principal is rebuffed by the superintendent.   RO SO O VFO
42. Teachers volunteer to help each other.   RO SO O VFO
43. The principal is effective in securing the superintendent's
    approval for new programs or activities.   RO SO O VFO
44. Academically oriented students in this school are ridiculed
    by their peers.   RO SO O VFO
45. Teachers do favors for each other.   RO SO O VFO

SOURCE: Kevin M. Barnes, *The Organizational Health of Middle Schools, Trust, and Decision Participation*. (Unpublished doctoral dissertation, Rutgers University, New Brunswick, New Jersey, 1994.) Used with permission.

Dimensions of Organizational Health
of Middle Schools (OHI-M)

Institutional Level

Institutional integrity describes a school that has integrity in its educational program. The school is not vulnerable to narrow, vested interests of community groups; indeed, teachers are protected from unreasonable community and parental demands. The school is able to cope successfully with destructive outside forces.

Administrative Level

Collegial leadership is behavior by the principal that is friendly, supportive, open, and guided by norms of equality. But at the same time, the principal sets the tone for high performance by letting people know what is expected of them.

Principal influence is the principal's ability to influence the actions of superiors. Influential principals are persuasive with superiors, get additional consideration, and proceed relatively unimpeded by the hierarchy.

Resource support refers primarily to classroom supplies and instructional materials. They are readily available; indeed, extra materials are supplied if requested.

Teacher Level

Teacher affiliation is a sense of friendliness and strong affiliation with the school. Teachers feel good about each other, their job, and their students. They are committed to both their students and their colleagues and accomplish their jobs with enthusiasm.

Academic emphasis is the extent to which the school is driven by a quest for academic excellence. High but achievable academic goals are set for students, the learning environment is orderly and serious, teachers believe in their students' ability to achieve, and students work hard and respect those who do well academically.

OHI-M

Organizational Health Inventory for Middle Schools

_____

900								
800								3%
700								
600								13%
								34%
500								
								34%
400								13%
300								
200								3%
100								
	Institutional Integrity	Collegial Leadership	Principal Influence	Resource Support	Teacher Affiliation	Academic Emphasis	Overall Health	

	Teachers' Perceptions	Principal's Perceptions
Institutional Integrity	_____	_____
Collegial Leadership	_____	_____
Principal Influence	_____	_____
Resource Support	_____	_____
Teacher Affiliation	_____	_____
Academic Emphasis	_____	_____
Overall Health	_____	_____

Hoy and Tarter. _The Road to Open and Healthy Schools: A Handbook for Change, Middle and Secondary School Edition._ Copyright © 1997, Corwin Press, Inc.

Appendix C
Instrument, Dimensions, and Profile Chart for OCDQ-RS

OCDQ-RS

Directions: The following are statements about your school. Please indicate the extent to which each statement characterizes your school by circling the appropriate response.

RO = rarely occurs; SO = sometimes occurs; O = often occurs; VFO = very frequently occurs

1. The mannerisms of teachers at this school are annoying.   RO SO O VFO
2. Teachers have too many committee requirements.   RO SO O VFO
3. Teachers spend time after school with students who have individual problems.   RO SO O VFO
4. Teachers are proud of their school.   RO SO O VFO
5. The principal sets an example by working hard himself or herself.   RO SO O VFO
6. The principal compliments teachers.   RO SO O VFO
7. Teacher-principal conferences are dominated by the principal.   RO SO O VFO
8. Routine duties interfere with the job of teaching.   RO SO O VFO
9. Teachers interrupt other faculty members who are talking in faculty meetings.   RO SO O VFO
10. Student government has an influence on school policy.   RO SO O VFO
11. Teachers are friendly with students.   RO SO O VFO
12. The principal rules with an iron fist.   RO SO O VFO
13. The principal monitors everything teachers do.   RO SO O VFO
14. Teachers' closest friends are other faculty members at this school.   RO SO O VFO
15. Administrative paperwork is burdensome at this school.   RO SO O VFO
16. Teachers help and support each other.   RO SO O VFO
17. Pupils solve their problems through logical reasoning.   RO SO O VFO
18. The principal closely checks teacher activities.   RO SO O VFO
19. The principal is autocratic.   RO SO O VFO
20. The morale of teachers is high.   RO SO O VFO
21. Teachers know the family background of other faculty members.   RO SO O VFO
22. Assigned nonteaching duties are excessive.   RO SO O VFO
23. The principal goes out of his or her way to help teachers.   RO SO O VFO
24. The principal explains his or her reason for criticism to teachers.   RO SO O VFO
25. The principal is available after school to help teachers when assistance is needed.   RO SO O VFO
26. Teachers invite other faculty members to visit them at home.   RO SO O VFO

OCDQ-RS (Continued)

27. Teachers socialize with each other on a regular basis.	RO	SO O	VFO
28. Teachers really enjoy working here.	RO	SO O	VFO
29. The principal uses constructive criticism.	RO	SO O	VFO
30. The principal looks out for the personal welfare of the faculty.	RO	SO O	VFO
31. The principal supervises teachers closely.	RO	SO O	VFO
32. The principal talks more than listens.	RO	SO O	VFO
33. Pupils are trusted to work together without supervision.	RO	SO O	VFO
34. Teachers respect the personal competence of their colleagues.	RO	SO O	VFO

SOURCE: John A. Mulhern, *The Organizational Climate of Secondary Schools: Revision of the OCDQ.* (Unpublished doctoral dissertation, Rutgers University, New Brunswick, New Jersey, 1984). Used with permission.

Dimensions of Organizational
Climate (OCDQ-RS)

Principal's Behavior

Supportive principal behavior is characterized by efforts to motivate teachers by using constructive criticism and setting an example through hard work. At the same time, the principal is helpful and genuinely concerned with the personal and professional welfare of teachers. Supportive behavior is directed toward both the social needs and task achievement of the faculty.

Directive principal behavior is rigid and domineering supervision. The principal maintains close and constant control over all teachers and school activities down to the smallest details.

Teachers' Behavior

Engaged teacher behavior is reflected by high faculty morale. Teachers are proud of their school, enjoy working with each other, and are supportive of their colleagues. Teachers are not only concerned about each other, they are committed to the success of their students. They are friendly with students, trust students, and are optimistic about the ability of students to succeed.

Frustrated teacher behavior refers to a general pattern of interference from both administration and colleagues that distracts teachers from the basic task of teaching. Routine duties, administrative paperwork, and assigned nonteaching duties are excessive; moreover, teachers irritate, annoy, and interrupt each other.

Intimate teacher behavior reflects a strong and cohesive network of social relationships among the faculty. Teachers know each other well, are close personal friends, and regularly socialize together.

Hoy and Tarter. *The Road to Open and Healthy Schools: A Handbook for Change, Middle and Secondary School Edition.* Copyright © 1997, Corwin Press, Inc.

OCDQ-RS

Organizational Climate Description Questionnaire for Secondary Schools

	Principal Behavior	Teacher Behavior	Openness
	Directive Behavior*	Frustrated Behavior*	
900	100	100	
800	200	200	3%
700	300	300	
600	400	400	13%
			34%
500	500	500	
			34%
400	600	600	13%
300	700	700	
200	800	800	3%
100	900	900	

| Supportive Behavior | Engaged Behavior | Intimate Behavior | School Openness |

* Reverse Scored

Teacher Perceptions		Principal Perceptions	
Principal- Supportive	_____	Principal- Supportive	_____
Principal- Directive*	_____	Principal- Directive*	_____
Teacher- Engaged	_____	Teacher- Engaged	_____
Teacher-Frustrated*	_____	Teacher- Frustrated*	_____
Teacher-Intimate		Teacher-Intimate	
School Openness	_____	**School Openness**	_____

Appendix D
Instrument, Dimensions, and Profile Chart for OHI-S

OHI-S

Directions: The following are statements about your school. Please indicate the extent to which each statement characterizes your school by circling the appropriate response.

RO = rarely occurs; SO = sometimes occurs; O = often occurs; VFO = very frequently occurs

1. Teachers are protected from unreasonable community and parental demands. RO SO O VFO
2. The principal gets what he or she asks for from superiors. RO SO O VFO
3. The principal is friendly and approachable. RO SO O VFO
4. The principal asks that faculty members follow standard rules and regulations. RO SO O VFO
5. Extra materials are available if requested. RO SO O VFO
6. Teachers do favors for each other. RO SO O VFO
7. Students in this school can achieve the goals that have been set for them. RO SO O VFO
8. The school is vulnerable to outside pressures. RO SO O VFO
9. The principal is able to influence the actions of his or her superiors. RO SO O VFO
10. The principal treats all faculty members as his or her equal. RO SO O VFO
11. The principal makes his or her attitudes clear to the school. RO SO O VFO
12. Teachers are provided with adequate materials for their classrooms. RO SO O VFO
13. Teachers in this school like each other. RO SO O VFO
14. The school sets high standards for academic performance. RO SO O VFO
15. Community demands are accepted even when they are not consistent with the educational program. RO SO O VFO
16. The principal is able to work well with the superintendent. RO SO O VFO
17. The principal puts suggestions made by the faculty into operation. RO SO O VFO
18. The principal lets faculty know what is expected of them. RO SO O VFO
19. Teachers receive necessary classroom supplies. RO SO O VFO
20. Teachers are indifferent to each other. RO SO O VFO
21. Students respect others who get good grades. RO SO O VFO
22. Teachers feel pressure from the community. RO SO O VFO
23. The principal's recommendations are given serious consideration by his or her superiors. RO SO O VFO
24. The principal is willing to make changes. RO SO O VFO
25. The principal maintains definite standards of performance. RO SO O VFO
26. Supplementary materials are available for classroom use. RO SO O VFO
27. Teachers exhibit friendliness to each other. RO SO O VFO
28. Students seek extra work so they can get good grades. RO SO O VFO
29. Select citizen groups are influential with the board. RO SO O VFO
30. The principal is impeded by superiors. RO SO O VFO

Hoy and Tarter. *The Road to Open and Healthy Schools: A Handbook for Change, Middle and Secondary School Edition.* Copyright © 1997, Corwin Press, Inc.

OHI-S (Continued)

31. The principal looks out for the personal welfare of faculty members.	RO SO O VFO
32. The principal schedules the work to be done.	RO SO O VFO
33. Teachers have access to needed instructional materials.	RO SO O VFO
34. Teachers in this school are cool and aloof to each other.	RO SO O VFO
35. Teachers in this school believe that their students have the ability to achieve academically.	RO SO O VFO
36. The school is open to the whims of the public.	RO SO O VFO
37. The morale of teachers is high.	RO SO O VFO
38. Academic achievement is recognized and acknowledged by the school.	RO SO O VFO
39. A few vocal parents can change school policy.	RO SO O VFO
40. There is a feeling of trust and confidence among the staff.	RO SO O VFO
41. Students try hard to improve on previous work.	RO SO O VFO
42. Teachers accomplish their jobs with enthusiasm.	RO SO O VFO
43. The learning environment is orderly and serious.	RO SO O VFO
44. Teachers identify with the school.	RO SO O VFO

SOURCE: John Feldman, *The School Health Index: The Development and Test of an Instrument Using a Parsonian and Etzonian Perspective.* (Unpublished doctoral dissertation, Rutgers University, New Brunswick, New Jersey, 1985.) Used with permission.

Dimensions of Organizational Health
of Secondary Schools (OHI-S)

Institutional Level

Institutional integrity describes a school that has integrity in its educational program. The school is not vulnerable to narrow, vested interests of community groups; indeed, teachers are protected from unreasonable community and parental demands. The school is able to cope successfully with destructive outside forces.

Administrative Level

Initiating structure is task- and achievement-oriented behavior. The principal makes his or her attitudes and expectations clear to the faculty and maintains definite standards of performance.

Consideration is principal behavior that is friendly, supportive, and collegial. The principal looks out for the welfare of faculty members and is open to their suggestions.

Principal influence is the principal's ability to influence the actions of superiors. The influential principal is persuasive, works effectively with the superintendent, and simultaneously demonstrates independence in thought and action.

Resource support refers to a school where adequate classroom and instructional materials are available and extra materials are easily obtained.

Teacher Level

Morale is the sense of trust, confidence, enthusiasm, and friendliness among teachers. Teachers feel good about each other and, at the same time, feel a sense of accomplishment from their jobs.

Academic emphasis refers to the school's press for achievement. High but achievable goals are set for students, the learning environment is orderly and serious, teachers believe students can achieve, and students work hard and respect those who do well academically.

Hoy and Tarter. *The Road to Open and Healthy Schools: A Handbook for Change, Middle and Secondary School Edition.* Copyright © 1997, Corwin Press, Inc.

OHI-S
Organizational Health Inventory for Secondary Schools

_____

	Institutional Integrity	Initiating Structure	Consideration	Principal Influence	Resource Support	Morale	Academic Emphasis	Overall Health	
900									
800									3%
700									
600									13%
									34%
500									
									34%
400									13%
300									
200									3%
100									

	Teachers' Perceptions	Principal's Perceptions
Institutional Integrity	_____	_____
Initiating Structure	_____	_____
Consideration	_____	_____
Principal Influence	_____	_____
Resource Support	_____	_____
Morale	_____	_____
Academic Emphasis	_____	_____
Overall Health	_____	_____

Hoy and Tarter. *The Road to Open and Healthy Schools: A Handbook for Change, Middle and Secondary School Edition.* Copyright © 1997, Corwin Press, Inc.

Appendix E
Computer Scoring Program Order Form and Data Report Form

Computer Scoring Program
Order Form

Name	
Institution	
Address	
City	
State	
Zip	
Phone	

	Price	Qty	Cost
Elementary School Package (OCDQ-RE & OHI-E)	$200.00		
Middle School Package (OCDQ-RM & OHI-M)	$200.00		
Secondary School Package (OCDQ-RS & OHI-S)	$200.00		
ALL THREE PACKAGES	$500.00		
Postage and Handling	3.00		
	Total		

Order by Mail or FAX

Arlington Writers Ltd.   FAX 614-488-5075
2548 Onandaga Drive   Pay by *Check*
Columbus, OH 43221   or attach a
                                      Purchase Order

Dear School Administrator:

We'd be interested in your results. If you'd be willing to share them with us, it will help us learn more about the climate of schools. All results are confidential—in fact, we have no place on the form for the name of the school or principal.

To send this form to us, just fold it, tape it shut, and stamp it, or place it in an envelope and send it to the address below.

Place
Postage
Stamp
Here

Dr. Wayne Hoy
The Ohio State University
29 W. Woodruff Ave.
Columbus, OH 43210-1177

All data pertains to the school. Approximate population and enrollment figures are adequate.

Country & Zip Code	State and Region of the Country
Population of the city or town where the school is located ____	Environment ____ Urban ____ Suburban ____ Rural
Number of students in the district ____	Grade levels in the school district ____ – ____
Number of students in your school ____	Grade levels in your school ____ – ____
Type and grade levels of your school ____ Middle School ____ Junior High ____ Secondary	Demographics ____ % African American ____ % Latino American ____ % Asian American ____ % European American ____ % Other

Scores on the OHI-M				Scores on the OHI-S			
Raw Scores		Standardized Scores		Raw Scores		Standardized Scores	
Overall Health		Overall Health		Overall Health		Overall Health	
II		II		II		II	
CL		CL		IS		IS	
PI		PI		PI		PI	
RS		RS		C		C	
TA		TA		RS		RS	
AE		AE		M		M	
				AE		AE	

Scores on the OCDQ-RM				Scores on the OCDQ-RS			
Raw Scores		Standardized Scores		Raw Scores		Standardized Scores	
Supportive		Supportive		Supportive		Supportive	
Directive		Directive		Restrictive		Restrictive	
Restrictive		Restrictive		Engaged		Engaged	
Principal Openness		**Principal Openness**		Frustrated		Frustrated	
Collegial		Collegial		Intimate		Intimate	
Committed		Committed					
Disengaged		Disengaged					
Teacher Openness		**Teacher Openness**		**School Openness**		**School Openness**	

References

Anderson, C. S. (1982). The search for school climate: A review of the research. *Review of Educational Research, 52*, 368-420.

Ashforth, S. J. (1985). Climate formations: Issues and extensions. *Academy of Management Review, 25*, 837-847.

Barnard, C. L. (1938). *Functions of the executive.* Cambridge, MA: Harvard University Press.

Bossert, S. T. (1988). School effects. In N. J. Boyan (Ed.), *Handbook of research on educational administration* (pp. 341-352). New York: Longman.

Brookover, W. B., Schweitzer, J. H., Schneider, J. M., Beady, C. H., Flood, P. K., & Wisenbaker, J. M. (1978). Schools, social systems and student achievement. *American Educational Research Journal, 15*, 301-318.

Carver, F. D., & Sergiovanni, T. J. (Eds.). (1969). *Organizations and human behavior: Focus on schools.* New York: McGraw-Hill.

Deal, T. E. (1985). The symbolism of effective schools. *Elementary School Journal, 85*, 601-620.

Deal, T. E., & Kennedy, A. (1982). *Corporate cultures.* Reading, MA: Addison-Wesley.

Dyer, W. G. (1985). The cycle of cultural evolution in organization. In R. H. Kilmann, M. J. Saxton, R. Serpa & Associates (Eds.), *Gaining control of the corporate culture* (pp. 200-230). San Francisco: Jossey-Bass.

Edmonds, R. R. (1979). Effective schools for the urban poor. *Educational Leadership, 37*, 15-24.

Forehand, G. A., & Gilmer, B. (1964). Environmental variation in studies of organizational behavior. *Psychological Bulletin, 62*, 361-381.

Frost, P. J., Moore, L. F., Louis, M. R., Lundberg, C. C., & Martin, J. (1985). *Organizational culture.* Beverly Hills, CA: Sage.

Gellerman, B. (1960). *People, problems, and profits.* New York: McGraw-Hill.

Gilmer, B. (1966). *Industrial psychology* (2nd ed.). New York: McGraw-Hill.

Halpin, A. W. (1966). *Theory and research in administration.* New York: Macmillan.

Halpin, A. W., & Croft, D. (1962, August). *The organizational climate of schools* (Research project, Contract No. SAE 543-8639). Washington, DC: U.S. Office of Education.

Halpin, A. W., & Croft, D. B. (1963). *The organizational climate of schools.* Chicago: Midwest Administration Center of the University of Chicago.

Hannum, J. (1994). *The organizational climate of middle schools, teachers efficacy, and student achievement.* Unpublished doctoral dissertation, Rutgers University.

Hannum, J., Hoy, W. K., & Sabo, D. (1996, April). *Organizational health and student achievement in middle schools.* Paper presented at the annual meeting of the American Educational Research Association, New York.

Hanson, P. G., & Lubin, B. (1995). *Answers to questions most frequently asked about organization development.* Thousand Oaks, CA: Sage.

Hoffman, J. D., Sabo, D., Bliss, J. R., & Hoy, W. K. (1994). Building a culture of trust. *Journal of School Leadership, 3,* x.

Hoy, W. K., Barnes, K., & Sabo, D. (1996). *The organizational health of middle schools: The concept and its measure.* Working paper, The Ohio State University, Public Policy and Educational Leadership.

Hoy, W. K., & Clover, S. I. R. (1986). Elementary school climate: A revision of the OCDQ. *Educational Administration Quarterly, 22,* 93-110.

Hoy, W. K., & Feldman, J. A. (1987). Organizational health: The concept and its measure. *Journal of Research and Development in Education, 20,* 30-38.

Hoy, W. K., & Ferguson, J. (1985). A theoretical framework and exploration of organizational effectiveness in schools. *Educational Administration Quarterly, 21,* 117-134.

Hoy, W. K., Hannum, J., & Sabo, D. (1996). *Middle school climate: An empirical assessment of organizational health and student achievement.* Working paper, The Ohio State University, Public Policy and Educational Leadership.

Hoy, W. K., Hoffman, J., Sabo, D., & Bliss, J. R. (1996). The organizational climate of middle schools: The development and test of the OCDQ-RM. *Journal of Educational Administration, 34,* 41-59.

Hoy, W. K., & Miskel, C. G. (1996). *Educational administration: Theory, research, and practice.* New York: Random House.

Hoy, W. K., & Sabo, D. (in press). *Quality middle schools: Open and healthy.* Thousand Oaks, CA: Corwin.

Hoy, W. K., Tarter, C. J., & Bliss, J. R. (1990). Organizational health, climate, and effectiveness: A comparative study. *Educational Administration Quarterly, 26,* 260-279.

Hoy, W. K., Tarter, C. J., & Kottkamp, R. B. (1991). *Open schools/healthy schools: Measuring organizational climate.* Newbury Park, CA: Sage.

Hoy, W. K., Tarter, C. J., & Witkoskie, L. (1992). Faculty trust in colleagues: Linking the principal with school effectiveness. *Journal of Research and Development in Education, 26(1),* 40-47.

Kilmann, R. H., Saxton, M. J., Serpa, R., & Associates (1985). *Gaining control of the corporate culture.* San Francisco: Jossey-Bass.

Kottkamp, R. B., Mulhern, J. A., & Hoy, W. K. (1987). Secondary school climate: A revision of the OCDQ. *Educational Administration Quarterly, 23,* 31-48.

Liao, Y. M. (1994). *School climate and effectiveness in Taiwan's secondary schools.* Doctoral dissertation, St. John's University, Queens, NY.

Litwin, G. H., & Stringer, R. A., Jr. (1968). *Motivation and organizational climate.* Boston: Division of Research, Harvard Business School.

Lorsch, J. W. (1985). Strategic myopia: Culture as an invisible barrier to change. In R. H. Kilmann, M. J. Saxton, R. Serpa, & Associates (Eds.), *Gaining control of the corporate culture* (pp. 84-102). San Francisco: Jossey-Bass.

Mackenzie, D. E. (1983). Research for school improvement: An appraisal of some recent trends. *Educational Researcher, 12,* 5-17.

Mayo, E. (1945). *The social problems of industrial civilization.* Boston: Graduate School of Business Administration, Harvard University.

Miles, M. (1965). Planned change in organizational health: Figure and ground. In F. D. Carver & T. J. Sergiovanni (Eds.), *Organizations and human behavior* (pp. 375-391). New York: McGraw-Hill.

Mintzberg, H. (1983). *Power in and around organizations.* Englewood Cliffs, NJ: Prentice Hall.

Miskel, C., Fevurly, R., & Stewart, J. (1979). Organizational structures and processes, perceived school effectiveness, loyalty, and job satisfaction. *Educational Administration Quarterly, 15,* 97-118.

Miskel, C., & Ogawa, R. (1988). Work motivation, job satisfaction, and climate. In N. J. Boyan (Ed.), *Handbook of research on educational administration* (pp. 279-304). New York: Longman.

Moos, R. (1979). *Evaluating educational environments.* San Francisco: Jossey-Bass.

Mott, P. (1972). *Characteristics of effective organizations.* New York: Harper & Row.

Ouchi, W. (1981). *Theory z.* Reading, MA: Free Press.

Ouchi, W., & Wilkins, A. L. (1985). Organizational culture. *Annual Review of Sociology, 11,* 457-483.

Pace, C. R., & Stern, G. C. (1958). An approach to the measure of psychological characteristics of college environments. *Journal of Educational Psychology, 49,* 269-277.

Parsons, T., Bales, R. F., & Shils, E. A. (1953). *Working papers in the theory of action.* Glencoe, IL: Free Press.

Pascale, R. T., & Athos, A. (1981). *The art of Japanese management.* New York: Simon & Schuster.

Peters, T., & Waterman, R. (1982). *In search of excellence: Lessons from America's best-run companies.* New York: Harper & Row.

Pettigrew, A. W. (1979). On studying organizational culture. *Administrative Science Quarterly, 24,* 570-581.

Purkey, S. C., & Smith, M. S. (1983). Effective schools: A review. *Elementary School Journal, 83,* 427-452.

Robbins, S. P. (1991). *Organizational behavior: Concepts, controversies, and applications.* Englewood Cliffs, NJ: Prentice Hall.

Rokeach, M. (1960). *The open and closed mind.* New York: Basic Books.

Rossman, G. B., Corbett, H. D., & Firestone, W. A. (1988). *Change and effectiveness in schools.* Albany: State University of New York Press.

Schein, E. H. (1985). *Organizational culture and leadership.* San Francisco: Jossey-Bass.

Schein, E. H. (1990). Organizational culture. *American Psychologist, 45,* 109-119.

Selznick, P. (1957). *Leadership in administration.* New York: Harper & Row.

Senge, P. (1990). *The fifth dimension: The art and practice of the learning organization.* New York: Doubleday.

Shouse, R. C., & Brinson, K. H., Jr. (1995, October). *Sense of community and academic effectiveness in American high schools: Some cautionary, yet promising evidence from NELS:88.* Paper presented at the annual meeting of the University Council for Educational Administration, Salt Lake City, Utah.

Stedman, L. C. (1987). It's time we changed the effective schools formula. *Phi Delta Kappan, 69*, 214-224.

Tagiuri, R. (1968). The concept of organizational climate. In R. Tagiuri & G. W. Litwin (Eds.), *Organizational climate: Explorations of a concept* (pp. 1-32). Boston: Division of Research, Graduate School of Business Administration, Harvard University.

Tarter. C. J., & Hoy, W. K. (1988). The context of trust: Teachers and the principal. *High School Journal, 72*, 17-24.

Tarter, C. J., Hoy, W. K., & Bliss, J. R. (1989). Principal leadership and organizational commitment: The principal must deliver. *Planning and Changing, 20*, 129-140.

Tarter, C. J., Sabo, D., & Hoy, W. K. (1995). Middle school climate, faculty trust, and effectiveness: A path analysis. *Journal of Research and Development in Education, 29*, 41-49.

Waldman, B. (1971). *Organizational climate and pupil control ideology of secondary schools.* Unpublished doctoral dissertation, Rutgers University, New Brunswick, NJ.

Wilkins, A. L., & Patterson, K. J. (1985). You can't get there from here: What will make culture-change projects fail. In R. H. Kilmann, M. J. Saxton, R. Serpa, & Associates (Eds.), *Gaining control of the corporate culture* (pp. 262-291). San Francisco: Jossey-Bass.

**CORWIN
PRESS**

The Corwin Press logo—a raven striding across an open book—represents the happy union of courage and learning. We are a professional-level publisher of books and journals for K–12 educators, and we are committed to creating and providing resources that embody these qualities. Corwin's motto is "Success for All Learners."